HARPER'S MAGAZINE PRESS

The Man Who Loved Bicycles

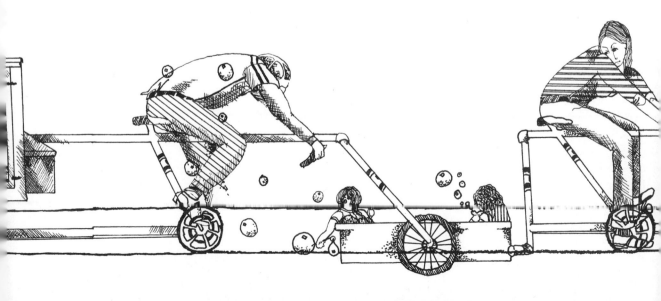

The Man Who Loved Bicycles

THE MEMOIRS OF AN AUTOPHOBE   by Daniel Behrman

Harper's Magazine Press
Published in Association with Harper & Row
New York

FIRST EDITION

Designed by Sheila Berger

Library of Congress Cataloging in Publication Data

Behrman, Daniel.
  The man who loved bicycles.

    1. Behrman, Daniel. I. Title.
CT275.B5565A3   301.31   72–12095
ISBN 0–06–120350–5

To *Botou-Koad*

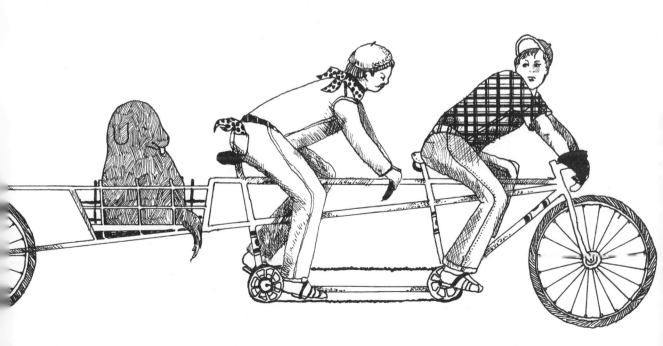

Contents

Chapter 1

SILENT SPRINGS OR, LOS ANGELES IS ANYWHERE

If, from time to time, this book is out-rageous, extravagant, and inconsistent, I will only be acknowledging the influence of the auto-huckster, whose claims pollute the newspapers and magazines I read daily. He claims without embarrassment that his product will do anything from curing athlete's foot to restoring sexual prowess. By the time the customer learns that it has restored his athlete's foot and cured his sexual prowess, the seller has moved down the river to deliver a new pitch about a new model that replaces hair and eliminates piles.

It's time the auto-huckster got a whiff of his own effluence. A few years ago, when a naïve publisher asked me to prospect a book on mass transit, I began to collect such memorabilia as National Academy of Science and National Research Council reports on motor vehicle emissions along with mind-boggling full-page ads from the leading car manufacturers of Europe and America. I call the publisher naïve because he was premature. One can miss the boat

just by turning up too soon. Eutrophication had not yet become a dirty fourteen-letter word, the environment was not yet the protégé of Atlantic Richfield and Standard Oil of New Jersey. I was just as naïve as he was. I went looking for support (read money) from various places on the strength of encouragement from a nice fellow in the Department of Transportation in Washington. His encouragement was hearty but mostly verbal; he seldom answered my letters. He just would not commit himself. When we talked in his office, he kept looking up as if at a much higher power. Only later did I learn what was bothering him. I came across an interview with his boss, John Volpe, then Secretary of the department and former Governor of Massachusetts. The Governor jogs on the roof of the Department of Transportation building in Washington, so I learned. He also rides an electric bicycle at home. He seemed to be a firm believer in exercise but not as a way to get somewhere. A quick workout on the electric bike, down to the office in the car, then up on the roof for a few laps. Governor, pull the plug on that bike, take it onto the towpath of the Chesapeake and Ohio Canal; the wilderness is almost at your door.

It was the publisher's original idea that I should ride transit systems, old and new, from San Francisco to New York, from BART to IRT, then talk to everyone closely or remotely concerned with the problem of mass transportation. I was to go from Lewis Mumford to Marshall McLuhan, from the cable car to the individualized personalized conveyor belt running from bedside to deskside on cheap convenient microwave energy beamed down from a satellite in stationary orbit. I had to study systems, said the nice fellow in his office at the Department of Transportation, old systems and new systems, all systems, trains, buses, cars.

The car a *transit system?* The more I looked at this system, the more it looked like an airline that was qualifying its people on Piper Cubs, then giving 747s and Concordes to pilots if they happened to be rich enough to buy them. From oilwell (whether troubling the oiled waters off Santa Barbara or deflating the earth when the crude is pumped out from underneath Colorado) to pipeline (try it on tundra) to refinery (especially downwind and, sooner or later, the wind always changes) to gas tank to exhaust pipe, it works as if it were designed as a *pollution system,* a form of chemical warfare we wage to defoliate our cities then our suburbs and our countryside, to interdict them all to the human race.

What's left over from the crude after the gasoline has been refined out is used to provide more boons at a cost the competition has no chance of meeting. DDT and other chlorinated hydrocarbons, for example. Our engines may be noisy but our springs are silent. Diesel oil, for another example. Trolleys go clang-clang-clang no more, instead we have the gas blast as the great GM bus roars off on its fifty-yard mission. We have the thirty-tonners racketing by everybody's front porch, putting everybody on the wrong side of the tracks; we have the diesel taxis in European cities that spread the choking blue haze of the open road into the most intimate urban nooks, where it stagnates, piling up like waste in an unflushed toilet. I will not get sentimental; I will say nothing of the living steam locomotives driven from the railroads by the oil-driven diesels, of the days when travel was a breath-catching adventure, when we needed only a ticket to take a trip, not a prescription. No, let us be practical and count the crumbs that the car gives us from the leavings of its table. Let us not forget petrochemicals, petrified chemicals, plastics in all their eternal forms. When they are new and bright, they drive out living materials: wood and leather, cotton and wool; when they are old and worn, they drive out life. Throw them away and they cover the countryside, the beaches, and the bottom of the sea. They neatly line the continental shelf. Burn them and they generate instant poison gas; chemical warfare all over again and within easy reach, no further away than the neighborhood dump.

And to what do we owe all these benefits, where should we direct our thanks? Why, to the car, of course. It oils the economy of the Western world. According to a providential article by Richard A. Rice, professor of transportation at Carnegie-Mellon University, who wrote it for MIT's *Technology Review,* transportation accounted for more than half of the 174 billion gallons of petroleum that the United States was using every year during the latter part of the Sixties. Private automobiles alone were burning about 60 billion gallons of petroleum a year. They may not have been carrying a full load of passengers, but they were certainly carrying the oil industry on their backs.

It is the car that puts the profit into drilling oil wells in such outlandish places as Alaska's North Slope or Europe's North Sea. It is the car that makes it worthwhile to air-condition the desert so that the oilmen can take their families with them to Araby. It is the car that makes it pay to build tankers a quarter of a mile long and send them around the Cape of Good Hope. The plastics and the insecticides, the fuel oil and the synthetic fabrics, they all get a free ride around the Cape. The cotton-grower and the cabinetmaker, the tanner and the sheep-raiser, they are all up against Ari.

Oil wins every time. Oil, cars, highways: that's where the winnings are. There is no need to break yet another lance against the depletion allowance or the top-heavy structure of American business with oil sitting on top. It is the richest industry in the United States; 91 leading oil corporations earned themselves $50 billion in 1969. It doesn't make much difference what Derby year one picks, the oil business always comes in first. It's bigger than automobiles, even though it is linked to them—one of a pair of inoperable Siamese twins.

It is no wonder that the oil industry gets the brightest people. At meetings of marine geologists—the kind of affairs of which I have some firsthand knowledge—you can always tell the oil-company men. They are the ones with the pressed suits and the tape recorders, the first to pick up a check and the last to publish their research results. They have infinite good humor—one of them is still on speaking terms with me after I told him he could be proud to work for BP—British Pollution. They may have sold their souls, but they got a good price.

I cannot see any great point in frothing at the mouth about the oil industry's position. At irregular intervals, the *New Republic* reaches me by sea mail in my Montparnasse quarters in Paris and tries to bring me to a boil about the monopoly of the oil barons or the tax loopholes that they enjoy. I do not boil. What does the *New Republic* want? Cheaper oil for the people, more smog for the masses? Nationalization of the oil emperors and their auto satrapies?

About three miles down the Seine from where I live there's the home plant of the biggest automobile manufacturer in France: Renault. It was nationalized nearly thirty years ago because Louis Renault collaborated with the Germans during the Second World War as a premature Common Marketeer. I don't know if any nationalized Renaults ever get recalled, but I do know that there's no chance of getting city hall to do anything about it. City hall *is* Renault. Don't expect to hear about dirty Renault exhausts on French television. City hall *is* television. Through what is known as "mixed" ownership (so mixed that no one can tell who owns what) the French government has a sizeable piece

4

of oil exploration and production in the Sahara and various other places. So lead in the gas is not a problem, and *emission* is a French word meaning a radio or TV broadcast, and just try to cut that down.

An unbelievable Paris paper, *Le Journal du Dimanche* (*Le Monde* is the only believable Paris paper) ran a story in 1970 about carbon monoxide pollution and concluded that "the situation is less perilous than one might have feared." It seems that cars put out the most carbon monoxide in Paris when they are idling. So there's really no problem, just set the carburetor so that the engine ticks at a clean idle . . . or race the motor all day long. "This method, applicable to all models, does not diminish the performance of vehicles and it costs nothing," says *Le Journal du Dimanche.* At least, this method cost Renault nothing in pollution-control expenses.

Apparently the sweet Parisian air (enriched by unfiltered exhausts) cleanses American cigarettes to the point where, just like the government-made Gauloises, they need carry no health warnings. The trouble with well-meaning socialism and nationalization is that it gets the state into evil businesses, which it costs too much to get out of, once the evil is discovered. The French government, according to another Paris paper, *France-Soir* (this one doesn't even believe itself, it changes its mind between editions), made almost a billion dollars making and selling tobacco in 1969 and about twice as much from taxes on gasoline and other petroleum products. That is why there is no Ralph Nader dubbed into French. When Nader gave a press conference in Paris and announced that about fifty thousand Renaults, Peu-

geots, and Simcas had failed to meet American safety requirements, he was simply ignored by the serious press. How do I know he announced it? It was reported in the *Canard Enchaîné,* a comic paper that runs the prime minister's income-tax returns as a regular feature, easily as funny as *Peanuts,* hardly distinguishable from *Pogo*.

This should be a lesson to the *New Republic* and others. All power to the people can make for an awful tangle when it comes to a separation of powers. There is only a smooth front, not a handhold can be seen in the monolithic face of the nationalized corporation. There is no way to scale it. What's good for Renault is good for the country because Renault *is* the country. Neither the German occupiers nor the American liberators touched a fraction of the precious stones of Paris that would be destroyed in a plan to put a mini-urban freeway along the Left Bank of the Seine. No need to look for the oil lobby or the highway lobby here, President Pompidou himself has been quoted as saying, "Paris must adapt to the automobile."

He is right. When it comes to moving people inside cities, the car must come first. The other entrants—subways, railroads, trolley cars, trolley buses, even that fourth cousin, the diesel bus—are in the transit business, the car is in the consuming business. That is why it is always ahead. Traffic jams use more gasoline and use up more cars, they must be preserved as living monuments of the free world. Free to do what? To build freeways and spread the jam around, to flatten the lumps into a smooth spread. The more freeways, the more cars; the more cars, the more jams; the more jams, the more freeways; and, not even paradoxically, the more subways, busways, and commuter railways.

There is a symbiosis here, though it cannot be detected at first. I got the scent of it when I came across an item in the *New York Times* to the effect that something like 115,000 cars come into Manhattan every day from Long Island and 25,000 from Westchester. Call it 200,000 people —each car is estimated to carry 1.3 persons (the .3 is the one that drives). Then what are we talking about? From the Bronx, from Brooklyn, from Queens, from uptown, they pour by the millions into Manhattan every morning on the subways. And 25,-000 from Westchester . . . on the Major Deegan Expressway, the Henry Hudson Parkway, the Connecticut Turnpike, the Sawmill River Parkway, the Merritt Parkway, the New York Thruway. Twenty-five thousand cars, 25 1,000-passenger subway trains, half an hour's work for two tracks. That is what all the bother and the pother is about . . . 25,000 cars from Westchester. This is not mass transit, friend, this is class transit.

Everybody has a car, everybody talks about his car, not everybody's going there by car. At least, not in the cities I know best, New York and Paris. Only when the subways and the Metro stop does the great beast crawl out of its burrow to blink its eyes, then unsheathe its rubber-clawed paws to mangle the *thruways* and the *autoroutes* (both words are in italics because they are foreign to the English language). Nothing moves, not even if it comes from Larchmont or Montfort-l'Amaury. It is then that the hubbub starts, ground is broken, the Second Avenue Subway rides again, the new Regional Métro flashes in from Saint-Germain-en-Laye to what used to be Place de l'Etoile, resting place of the Unknown Soldier, until it was renamed Place Charles de Gaulle in honor of a well-known general.

Too little transit and the old cars come out of hiding and into use, the Edsels and the Packards, the Simca Arondes and the Dyna Panhards, wheels for the people. When the motormen on the Paris Métro go on strike, the motors go to work. The buzzing smoking inching junk oozes through the gates of Paris, freezes during the day, thaws in the evening, and oozes out again. Every day, the brown stain over the city gets thicker, another layer is added, it is visible another ten miles out on clear sunny days. The Métro motormen only strike on clear sunny days, they never get their weather forecasts wrong, they must keep the pedestrians on their side. So it is the good weather that is bad, it is the bad weather that is good. The west wind that brings the rain in from the coast of Normandy flushes the brown stain from the city's sky, it washes the carbon monoxide from the streets, it is an emergency whiff of oxygen. There is something to breathe until the wind reverses again and the air grows still over the valley of the Seine, trapped by the low hills that mount in the west toward Versailles. One need only to look at the Impressionists to see what has happened to the air of Paris. They were able to get the dappling of light on the city when steam from the first trains out of Saint-Lazare station shuttered the sun so that it striped them in gold. Not any more, Monet, not any more. The sun turns Paris gray, Paris turns the sun into an overcooked fried egg, brown and sickly. The

Eiffel Tower might be rising to infinity, no one can see where it ends.

Paris might as well be Los Angeles. Thank God for Los Angeles; no matter how crudded a city may be, there is always Los Angeles and its peculiar inversion, easily seen in local mores and clothes. Everyone is always better off than the Angelinos. Serves them right, too, all those movie stars and sunshine, it was too good to be true, retribution was bound to find Los Angeles. A scare lead in a British paper, the *Sunday Times* of London: " 'She has not lived in Los Angeles long,' said a coroner, reporting on a recently found body. 'Her lungs are barely damaged.' Los Angeles is unique—its cars poison more people than do those of any other city."

Further along in the text that went with the Englishman's Sunday roast:

> *Because British towns are generally gloomy as well as draughty, the unburnt hydrocarbons in the exhaust gas are relatively unimportant. . . . Exhaust gases always contain partially burnt hydrocarbons. Sunshine turns these into a mixture that damages the lungs and causes weeping, and sunny California, in particular, suffers this way. This is the principal reason why cars for export to the United States must now be fitted with devices to complete the combustion of the exhaust gases.*

Tommyrot . . . balderdash . . . waffle. Is this the *Sunday Times* or *Le Journal du Dimanche*? Perhaps it's *Le Times du Dimanche*. Smog must be a foreign disease, an extrainsular affliction that strikes down all those, and it is not greatly to their credit, who are not Englishmen. Nothing good ever comes from abroad, the rain on the French Riviera arrives on "the wind from Italy," the Spanish disease struck down Casanovas everywhere except in Spain, smog is as alien and un-British as sunshine. Oh, is it? A quote from another London Sunday read, *The Observer*—a story dated February 20, 1972, and trumpeted by Jeremy Bugler, their Environment Correspondent:

> *Widespread repercussions are expected from the disclosure that Los-Angeles-type photochemical smog was found in the South of England last summer.*
>
> *Three scientists from the Atomic Energy Research Establishment at Harwell, Berkshire, have proved for the first time that photochemical smog has occurred in Britain's atmosphere. The report of their finding appears in the current issue of* Nature.
>
> *"These are most important results,"* said John Reay, head of the air pollution division of Warren Springs, Stevenage, the Government pollution laboratories, *"We shall now have to take seriously the smog problem in Britain."*
>
> *The smog occurs when car exhaust fumes are exposed to strong sunlight, setting off a chemical reaction. At one stroke, the scientists, Dr. Dick Atkins, Dr. Tony Cox and Dr. Alan Eggleton, have destroyed the widely held view that photochemical smog could not occur here because Britain has less sunlight than, for example, California.*
>
> *The scientists set up their instruments in a first-floor Harwell laboratory. They measured the concentration of ozone over a period of 35 days. The presence of certain levels of ozone is considered*

by United States Government experts to be evidence of photochemical smog.

On six days they found ozone levels that reached or exceeded the safety levels recommended in the U.S. "On two of these days, we found the ozone above the level at which smog is known to cause eyes to smart," said Dr. Eggleton, "and this was out in the countryside, not in the towns."

So Los Angeles is anywhere. No airport rush, no reservations, as soon as the cars and the sun come out together, instant Los Angeles. Even on the sidewalks of New York.

A dip into my clips and up comes an interview with Dr. Robert N. Rickles, Commissioner of Air Resources (both of them) for the city. He was recorded by *The New Yorker* as saying: "There is evidence that people living near freeways in Los Angeles accumulate lead in their tissues, and we know that the levels of lead that have been measured out there are lower than those on some of our streets. Our levels are really pretty high."

Here we are being preposterous, we are mixing photochemical smog and lead poisoning. So let's be outrageous and throw some oil in as well. Dr. Rickles was also worried by a city bus garage on Staten Island.

"Apparently, they have inadequate space over there for all their old diesel-engined buses, and they've been afraid to leave them out at night for fear the engines won't start in the morning so they've been running them—as many as seventy-five of them, by our count—all night long. We know of fifty families who live in private houses just fifty to sixty

feet from those buses, and we can document cases of kids who haven't been able to go to school because they've been made sick by those exhausts. Now just how long are we supposed to tolerate this sort of insult to our people?"

Until the horse cars come back, no doubt, Commissioner, and there will always be an oil flak to shed a tear for the poor kids who will be kept awake all night by the neighing. If the lead doesn't get you, then the diesels must. Anything that doesn't run on oil gets run out. Cars run on oil, but they run better on lead. Between 1946 and 1968, according to a figure that Barry Commoner left lying around loose in *The Closing Circle,* the amount of lead cars needed to run 1,000,000 miles went up from 280 to 500 pounds and the total that went up into the air from 50,000 to 260,-000 tons every year. As my friend from British Petroleum once put it to me, people must decide whether or not they want high-performance cars. Or low-performance people.

Or growth. The effect of the car on the economy is read most easily perhaps in the pollution indices. The most conservative estimate I ever saw, courtesy of U.S. Public Health, blames 60 percent of the air pollution in the country on the car, with industry providing 17 percent and electric power plants 14 percent. But what is industry making most of? Cars. Where does an unidentified but certainly large chunk of the electric power go? Automobile plants, for one. For another, air conditioning; the smoggier the air, the more it needs conditioning.

Come and wander with me along the

8

motor trail. Let your imagination go, don't just stick your nose up in the air, get it down near the water. Salt water first. The fish off southern California are swimming around with twice as much lead as the fish off Peru. Fresh (ha!) water next. Bugler, our Environment Correspondent in the *Observer* of London, took a stroll along the River Irwell that fumes through Manchester, among other places in industrial Lancashire. "If you fall in the Irwell, you will be rushed to hospital and stomach-pumped." What does the poor automobile have to do with the Irwell? Directly, nothing. Indirectly, draw your own conclusions. Lancashire Steel is on the river; if they're not producing for the car industry, they probably wish they were. Right on the other bank of the Irwell, enters the Mersey with a load of oil and chemical waste from Shell Chemicals. Let's amble downstream with Bugler. To your left, the Berry Wiggins refinery and oil waste, to your right the Burmah Oil refinery and more you-know-what. Some oil spillage from an Esso tank farm a little further on and here we are at Electric Power Storage, producing Exide batteries and lead pollution. No one is making sexy Minis (Morris or Austin) on the banks of the Irwell, but that is why the refineries and the battery plant are there.

And the jobs. Drive the automobile into a corner and it will always reverse out. Sure we're dirty, but look at all the good we do, the millions we support. Knock out the prop of the car and the whole country falls flat on its face. Or if you prefer, more polite language by Earl Cook in *Scientific American:* "We could not now make any major move toward a lower per capita energy consumption without severe economic dislocation."

At the risk of being un-American, I shall be unscientific. What have we been going through during the past few years if not severe economic dislocation? What kind of jobs do oil and cars provide? What about quantity? A figure comes to mind; the French want to spend 600 million francs (about $132 million the last time I looked at a paper) to put in a big refinery complex on the coast near Brest and bring jobs to Brittany. Six hundred, to be precise, $220,000 per job; the interest alone would be enough to give each man a handsome annuity without lousing up the Bay of Brest. Or else the money could be used to subsidize those underdeveloped Western European countries that do not make cars. The French could send food packages to Switzerland and warm clothes to Norway and Denmark. Belgium could come in for a share of the aid, so could Sweden and Holland with their relatively small-sized car factories. With the money, the Swiss could then build expressways in the Alps and close down outmoded electric railroads running at all hours of the day and night, even through snow and ice, when people should be sitting home and planning their next year's vacations. The Danes could widen their roads to engulf the bicycle paths that now run alongside them, they could reduce their ridiculous taxes on cars so that drivers would change them more often instead of nursing along Plymouths or Opels old enough to vote.

As for the kind of jobs that the car business provides, it's high time we talked about the quality of work along with all of our blather about the quality of life. People like to identify with their work, it is the way they have always defined themselves, the Millers and the Wainwrights, the Smiths and the Carters. They don't seem to be able to identify with making automobiles, they would rather not be concerned with the crafting of the 6,700,000 Chevrolets that came out between 1965 and 1969 with defective engine mounts or the Volkswagens that teeter in a high wind or the Morris Marina of a Mr. Derek Pope that, in the space of nine months, required a new gearbox, exhaust system, alternator, front brake linings and drums, two front seats, four door locks, glove compartment lock, steering column lock . . . no need to continue, but I could.

Automobile plants are much better at making a fuss. This is the industry where mass production of heavy consumer goods began; it was in the automobile plants that the CIO and industrial unionism got their start. Coming down from ancient to more current history, it was in a Renault plant in Normandy that the tragic farce of May 1968 began when some young Maoists on the line decided to occupy the factory. Renault pays the best wages in the French auto industry, it has the newest plants, they probably are nice places to live in as long as no one has to work there. The Renault hands lived in their plants for over a month in 1968, not even their union could get them out.

Closer to the present, there is the spate of what the *New York Times* has called "blue collar blues," heard mainly in the automobile plants. At Ford, GM, and Chrysler, Agis Salpukas said in an article in the *Times,* absenteeism went up from between 2 and 3 percent in 1965 to 5 to 6 percent at present, and it can go as high as 15 percent on Fridays and Mondays, thereby making for a four-day or even a three-day week. We are supposed to keep driving automobiles because they create jobs, but who wants the jobs? Not too many people at Chrysler in 1969; almost half of them couldn't get through their first three months. That was the year that 8 percent of Oldsmobile's Wixom plant near Detroit was quitting every month. "This meant that 4,300 workers had to be hired every year to maintain a work force of 5,000." The *Times* reporter went out into the field and interviewed hands who were getting through the day by bringing bottled lunches, whiskey or wine. The reporter listened. "I don't know what it is they can do, but they have to change these jobs. If you don't get a break off that line, you can go crazy. . . . Each year, I felt like I accomplished something. Suddenly I realized that I'm at a dead end and I'll probably be hacking on the line for 30 years." Suddenly, the *Times* reader learns that making cars can be as boring, dull, and deadening a way to pass time as driving them. There is not much hope of a change. He reads on: "Proposals such as having teams of workers build one car or a large unit, or having workers follow one car along the assembly line are considered impractical by auto executives and even some union leaders. Douglas Fraser, the head of the UAW's Chrysler department, said: 'If you tripled plant capacity and would be willing to pay $10,000 per car, then you could have teams build cars.'" The production line really came into being in automobile plants; first it got the worker, then it got the customer; it has got all of us who are around cars, we all lead production-line lives.

Not necessarily. There is a way out without spending $10,000 for a car. About twelve years ago, I spent $10 for a used bike in Paris. Never buy a used bike from anyone; the model has not changed since 1903, there is no plausible reason why anyone should get rid of a good bike. The one I bought was ageless; the seat quickly gave way to reveal that it had been concocted of rubber painted to look like leather. That bike had gone through the Occupation, but I was not ready to make a proper investment. I only needed a bike to pedal around the Bois de Boulogne. The man who used to rent bikes outside the Bois had given up, he had converted his shop into a service station. So I acquired my venerable black bike. I didn't dare ride it in the streets of Paris, I stuffed it into the back of the car and drove it, like an invalid, to the Bois de Boulogne where we could take the air together on a bike path all of a mile and a half long. I was a secret cyclist; no one in the *quartier* knew of my old black bike.

Then the Métro went on strike. As usual, the nationalized electric-power workers went out at the same time. The traffic lights went off. At every intersection, the French rules of the road applied: driver on the right has the right of way, he has top *priorité* going into the intersection and none at all getting out. He comes in like a lion, he goes out on tiptoes . . . if he is lucky, if the Métro is not on strike and people he would never dream of associating with are not using their cars. If they are

out, then he does not go out at all. Cars clog the crossing concentrically like tree rings until they reach the sidewalk, they mount the curb, now they swirl more slowly as in a sink with a plugged drain, they overflow to the building line, the swirl stops.

That was how I found Carrefour Vavin on the morning of the Métro strike when I took my car from the garage and set out to work. There is a painting of Carrefour Vavin in the Montparnasse of the Twenties; people are dancing on the fourteenth of July there where Boulevard du Montparnasse meets Boulevard Raspail, where Gertrude Stein and Ernest Hemingway and William Faulkner met on the terrace of the Dôme after the First World War, where American students in Paris on the GI Bill of Rights used to sit after the Second World War, one of them mounting guard to spot the big Ford of the Veterans Administration attaché at the embassy who drove around checking attendance in the cafés because the French refused to check it in the classrooms.

The morning of the Métro strike, the steel and rubber flood had washed away all traces of Hemingway and Faulkner, of the table at the Coupole where we used to take a *café liègeois,* letting my infant son lap up the whipped cream, of the table at the Dôme that caught the sun at breakfast time in the empty Paris of August.

I backed the car into the garage and took the rusty black bike out of a corner where it was gathering dust. I walked it through Carrefour Vavin, I swung into the saddle, the springs squeaked, my muscles creaked. I was not used to such violent exercise with a charcoal suit, a black raincoat, and a briefcase, the *accoutrement* that I favored in my attempt to pass unnoticed among the Parisians who go around all year long as if they were going to a funeral, their brows frowning, their eyes set on the thin blue line of the Vosges standing between them and their next vacations, the vacations that stand between them and retirement.

Beyond Carrefour Vavin, the road was clear. There were no cars to be seen on Boulevard du Montparnasse, Carrefour Vavin was clinging to them like an Auvergnat to a gold *louis*. I had the road all to myself right to Montparnasse station, where Charybdis had been at work again, another whirlpool that had to be skirted high and on the outside, then it was all downhill to my destination at the Organization, the captor of my labors. Ten minutes from start to stop, a mile and a half from door to door, the wrought-iron door of my apartment house near the Luxembourg Gardens, the plate-glass door of the Organization. Six minutes was the best I had ever done by car and that was only coming home for a late lunch when I was alone on the street and everyone else was putting down a second *apéritif* prior to starting on the wine. Three-quarters of an hour was my worst time, it was at six o'clock on a Friday night just prior to one of those big neap tides when the city of Paris ebbs to the provinces, when everyone takes his car, not just those who can afford to drive. Then the trip had to be planned all day long; gas, water, and battery checked; alternate routes memorized; food, drink, and reading matter taken aboard.

On the bike, I was above it all. I surveyed everything from my high perch as I used to look down on New York from the open top deck of a Fifth Avenue bus. The old black bike wasn't as high as a double-decker bus, but cars had gotten a lot flatter since I was young. From my crow's nest, I could see the village-sized Paris I had known right after the war, when there was only one car to be seen for a mile around and it was mine. The city shrank, my perspective lengthened, my world was no longer limited to the runways where I could land my car.

My romance with the automobile was ending, that great American love story was almost over. I had been first smitten at innocent seventeen when I got a Michigan driver's license that I could display in New York when I came home on school vacations, a pseudo-farm boy. I have had New York driver's licenses now for long past thirty years, never a black mark to my name and no wonder: I do all my driving in France. As for the French driver's license, I got it in 1948 for life. It never needs to be renewed, there are no physical examinations, I can go on driving with it after death into the great beyond.

The first car I ever owned was a '47 Chevrolet, light tan, two-door sedan. The next year, I came to Europe; the Chevy paid our passage over with enough left for a black Citroën when we got here. It was the first of a series of Citroëns, part of my ludicrous attempt to blend into the landscape, a black Citroën and brown Gauloises. Every Parisian I met in those days was trying to get his hands on a Plymouth and a pack of Chesterfields.

I still own a '69 Citroën; it stays in a garage for weeks on end. It comes out only to serve as a bike carrier, a first-stage bike launcher. I use it as the eleventh speed (eighty miles per hour) on a ten-speed bicycle to get out of the foul-air zone around Paris while admittedly fouling the air some more in the process. I take the bike out in the car as a last resort, when I have had all that I can stand of the imitation countryside of city parks and squares with their varnish of unburnt hydrocarbons and their day-long Muzak from the passing mufflers. Then the bike goes into the trunk of the car; the Citroën looks like it is trying to swallow it all except for an indigestible front wheel, and I roll out to the forest of Fontainebleau or Rambouillet. I stop the car, I break out the bike, and I am off through the woods, a wheeled deer, the brakes jutting out like antler branches from the racing handlebars. The air bites, the oxygen gets into blood and brain, the wheels sing on the narrow strip of a tarred forest lane, an idea comes to mind.

And that is how I have done this writing: I get on my bike and I get mad. This piece is written as much in passion as in reason. I am an old hand at science writing, I know how to check a fact to a frazzle and weasel my words to the satisfaction of the most worrisome source. But not this time, for once let the burden of proof be on the other side.

Chapter 2

THE DEADLY MUSTANG-COUGAR-JAGUAR-TIGER GT WHEELCHAIR

Car-lifting the bike is the only way I know to beat the syndrome of city living. The whole thing works as if it were masterminded by Dr. Fu Manchu or Moriarty; it works so well that it can't be accidental. The more you drive, the less air there is to breathe, the less air there is to breathe the more you have to drive because you are just not capable of doing anything else. Heaven help you if you try.

Back in bad old Los Angeles, I understand people are told to stay home and do nothing during air-pollution alerts. I learned this by reading a Paris newspaper —the best way to learn what is wrong with Los Angeles and the rest of the United States. But no Paris newspaper has yet gotten around to explaining to me why I spit black solid particles in Paris and nowhere else, not even in New York. Paris was once civilized, now it's dieselized. It is when I start spitting black that I sound my own alert; I cut my effort down to the point of doing nothing more than wiggling the steering wheel of my Citroën until I

have gotten up up and the hell away.

But don't let the exhaust fool you, it's only a smoke screen. Run an automobile on steam, electricity, sunshine, or the morning dew, it'll still get you. Put on bumpers of eiderdown, bring back the man on horseback waving a red flag ahead of every motorcar (why did they ever take him away?), the automobile will still be lethal.

For that deadly Mustang-Cougar-Jaguar-Tiger GT you take by the tail is really nothing but a wheelchair. The difference is that most wheelchairs give the patient a chance to push the wheels. Hardly a wheel to push or turn in the deadly Mustang-Cougar-Tiger etc., it demands no more effort than the paraplegic's eyelid flick that flips the pages of an electrically operated book. A buddy of mine who had a foot nerve severed in the infantry got a priority in 1945 for an Olds Hydramatic; everybody has a priority today. Everybody is a paraplegic, we have superpower for infra-people.

Rewrite the riddle of the Sphinx, cut the

legs out from under it. What starts out in life on wheels and stays on wheels until wheeled out? What starts out in a carriage, graduates to a stroller, then walks only through childhood and early adolescence until carried again by wheels? Why, it is man the hunter, that two-legged beast of prey. He could run a horse into the ground, he could plow a hundred acres, take a reef off Cape Horn, shovel four tons of coal on a single shift, he could do all of that and more. Not any more. Now he sits and twitches a finger and a toe. Yet his genes and his metabolism have not changed during the nanosecond of his biological history that has seen him reduced to a lump of helpless cushioned cosseted flesh.

He goes on eating like the hunter and the plowman, the *boeuf bourguignon* of the peasant winegrower, the *bouillabaisse* of the fisherman, the lumberjack's flapjacks, the cowboy's steaks, and he does nothing at all. Again the syndrome; the more he eats, the bigger the car he needs to be able to move. He can pass on a hill at eighty miles per hour, but he can't climb a flight of stairs. This is where the car gets us; we are turned into a nation of Falstaffs but only superficially. We are not jovial fat men, we're just fat. The pot belly and the beefy jowls of the Victorian exploiter of child labor, we've all got them now, the exploiters and the exploited, a classless society all in the same weight class. Everyone looks like Diamond Jim Brady, but it doesn't come from high living with Lillian Russell.

Small wonder that the organism of man the hunter races wildly; all that energy intake is going wild, Achilles' heel is on the accelerator, his toe is on the brake. Small

wonder that the energy bursts out elsewhere; perhaps it erupts into carcinomas that strike us down willy-nilly like the plague in Defoe's London, you're here today, you're gone tomorrow. It cloaks us, too, with unhealthy tissue, a refuse heap of quivering grease that we must tote with us when we jelly out of our wheelchairs, our hearts pumping like a schoolgirl's at the sight of her first swain, our chests heaving, our lungs panting.

A preposterous outrageous claim. Of course it is but go take it apart. Find a controlled population identical in all respects except that some drive cars and some do not. Keep tabs on them from adolescence on, prove beyond a shadow of a doubt that the disease pattern for the drivers is the same as that of the carless, that the incidence of cancer is identical or, at least, within the bounds of statistical error. Even if you succeeded, I wouldn't believe you because it doesn't suit me. It did not suit a number of people to believe the Surgeon General when he produced his report on smoking, based on patients living the same lives in veterans' hospitals except that some used cigarettes and some did not. But don't worry, the tests are being run now, everyone is in the experiment whether he likes it or not, no one is asking him, we have been volunteered. What is it that knocks the growth process askew, that disturbs the balance of regulatory mechanisms? We do not know, of course, there are so many factors; some may be self-canceling, others are certainly synergistic. What we do know is that no human beings until now have ever commanded so much artificial energy while using so little of their own.

The calories pour into the gut; the gasoline that goes into the tank is converted into motion, but not the calories in the gut. The power has to be used up, it has to go somewhere. Smoking is one way. I do not know the physiology, all I do know is that I was a lot more tired when I smoked. I did much less, I needed sleep more than I do now. Tobacco can use up the excess energy. Yet it, too, seems to spoil the balancing act. For a while, we can do anything, smoke, drive, eat, drink. Not forever, though; the furnace stops drawing, we keep shoveling the stuff in but it doesn't go away. Cut down on sweets, try cyclamates instead; no, back to saccharine again; anything that will save the sweet sensation of fuel going down the gut without forcing us to convert it to work. Try the drinking man's diet, try the driving man's diet.

That is the true physical pollution of the car. The maimed and the dead are the tip of the iceberg, the gassed and the poisoned are but part of the picture. The real loser is the winner, the man who, like my late, dear father, never has an accident, never

is hit, just sits and swells in his driver's seat, from Willys-Overland to LaSalle, over the years his engines growing more and more powerful as he grows weaker and weaker. It was the second infarctus that got my dad. After the first, he watched the cholesterol, he stopped smoking, he thinned down until the confidence came back, he started driving again, eating again, taking a taxi four blocks to the office. He thought he was whole again; he was moving less than when I had walked him slowly through the Bagatelle Gardens in the Bois de Boulogne after the first heart attack that had hit him in Europe. And he died, he survived his own father by only two years. The old man had faded at eighty-nine. I think his last car must have been a Franklin and he got rid of it when it was almost new. He walked through the jungles of Manhattan unafraid, he lived on the edge of Harlem where he had moved up from the Lower East Side as a young man; he smoked to the end; he outdrank three generations; he never used anything more

than a cane to move about. He was a sport and a sportsman. Fifty years ago he visited a ranch in Wyoming, he had kept horses and women; he went deep-sea fishing with his cronies who kept their derbies on as they dropped their lines and hoisted their glasses. He looked you straight in the eye with a flask in his hand, straight with his untamed eyes. He was a pre-car man, my grandfather, he lived but he did not talk of his living.

He was a sport in the day before the advent of the sport car, that contradiction in terms, the overhead-cammed, mid-engined, wide-tired wheelchair for the dead tired. I won't malign the pro, the rally driver who does it for a living. I once rode with Jean Vinatier of the Renault stable around the road circuit at Montlhéry outside Paris. He took me with him for some kind of a story that I had to do. He did a day's work; I remember he had forearms thick as telegraph poles, they moved the wheel at just the right moment to throw us into a power skid. We drifted around the turns of Montlhéry without a swerve, the Renault sideslipping easily, power holding it in place, wheels cocked at the right angle to keep us sliding. Then the forearms moved just ever so little and we were rolling down a straight, moving up to a hundred miles per hour until down went his foot and the smell of brake pads rose up again. Vinatier was risking only his own life; I felt safer with him than on Route Nationale 20, the Paris-Orléans highway that I had taken out to Montlhéry. No one was watching us, no one was listening, he was keeping his touch, running through the scales. That was sport driving, it had nothing to do with laying rubber on Boulevard

Saint-Germain before the impassive eyes of some poor *agent* who knows that anyone who can afford a Porsche can fix a ticket . . . and fix the wagon of some poor *agent* along with it.

The sport car is nothing but plastic surgery; the older and uglier one gets, the leaner and younger one's car must look. The pudgy and the puffy are turned into svelte long-muscled youths with the barrel chests of four-barreled carburetors, the tapering limbs of flared tailpipes. The car is a face; how many times have I been told that I did not see an acquaintance who drove by me in a red Peugeot 204 while I was on a bicycle. Yvonne saw me on a bicycle, I saw only the red Peugeot 204; it could have been Yvonne, it could have been the pharmacist on Rue Brea, it could have been anyone completely hidden, anonymous, nameless behind the huge mask of the windshield. It could have been a red Peugeot 204 driven by a computer and guided by radar, an experimental model intended to test the neuromotor responses demanded by traffic on Rue d'Assas. The only drivers I know by their vehicles are a few truckmen: Feron, the moving man, with the special high green body he put on a Mercedes-Benz chassis; Gasq, the coalman, a flatbed Citroën truck bowed under coal sacks. These men use motors to work, not to consume, they do not buy them as disguises.

That is how the pudgy and the puffy wear their Jaguars and their Citroën Maseratis in Paris. Their wives seem to favor Fiat 850s or sawed-off Peugeots as if, unlike the menfolk who try to present a face of power, they want to look winsome and *petite*. The heart of the little Fiat is young and gay even if Madame is old and sad, sadder and wiser with the knowledge of what Monsieur is up to with the E-type Jaguar, all hood and engine, a four-wheeled phallus, more plastic surgery, the ultimate prosthesis.

I know a great deal has been thought and written about the bumper guards of Cadillacs during the Fifties and the thrust of hood ornaments, but even that aspect of the automobile is illusory. A friend of mine, Serge Vitry, once let me drive his steam locomotive. I sat in his chair, I looked out the window, there was the boiler, black, thirty feet long, shooting orange flame at one end, spouting steam at the other, whistling in the middle. I told him about the symbolism, he had never heard of it. He didn't know what I was talking about, he let me shout my inanities while he kept an eye on the water gauge and the track. Not many E-type Jaguars would be sold if a few more people could have a chance to watch a steam engine cleave the countryside, leaving it quiet and contented after the train has gone, the leaves hardly trembling in their repose, a caress of love, not at all the gang-shag of the superhighway, the perpetual day-and-night flashing of the putative Vinatiers in their sport cars. What a strange sport, there is none like it; men of fifty do not buy football helmets to go out and emulate Joe Namath, but anyone can buy Vinatier's Alpine and, in France, drive it legally as fast as Vinatier does. In America, cooler heads prevail; the car is meant to be seen rather than heard, the Toronado and the Le Mans purr along at the same quiet rate as the laundry trucks and the campers. Americans belt up in their sport cars, they are trussed like

sausages, wrapped like packages, physically fit only to be tied. Yes, the car has given us mobility. On some cars, the trouble with the safety belt is that it makes it hard to reach the hand brake and the hand brake is the last aspect of automobility that demands any effort at all.

So we are bound hand and foot to our sport cars, we seal ourselves in, we drop into the box, we have all the mobility of a letter except that it can go first-class. We go fourth-class, junk mail, containerized bulk shipments. We can't even go to the toilet, no stopping except at designated rest areas. We have true mobility, eternal mobility, we are condemned like the wandering Jew to wander from one rest area to another, to beat like the Flying Dutchman around the Hawthorne Circle or the Bagnolet interchange. The British scream blue murder because steers can't turn around on factory farms, yet it is the British who pen humans into MGs and Morgans where they can hardly move enough to glance in a rear-view mirror, let alone turn their heads. I once interviewed a pioneer of the research submersible; he could not understand why people were reluctant to cram themselves into spherical pressure hulls no more than six feet in diameter. "It's not nearly as uncomfortable as going from Boston to New York in a Volkswagen." The airlines hesitated before they tried to sell us the big economy-sized box of a 747. They were wrong, they should put their tallest passenger model into the back seat of a two-door import and redesign their seats around him.

As it is, there is hardly any difference between driving to and flying from an air-

18

port. In both cases, the passenger is fastened to his seat and various distractions must be placed at his disposal to stop him from reminding himself that he can be dead at the next moment before he even has time to change the stereo tape cartridge or put on his earphones to catch the dialogue of the mature film. Planes and cars alike need entertainment: in-flight movies put seeing back into flying, rear-seat television is apparently on its way in cars. Only the driver will be deprived of a view of the world outside. He will have to be content with what he can glimpse of his passengers' expressions in his mirror as they watch the show. He always has the same view through the windshield, he only has to keep track of the exit numbers; never have people traveled so much and seen so little. The car started as a way to go places, it soon became a place.

While the commercial airliner is only an occasional experience, even for the seasoned passenger, the car is a semi-permanent environment. It influences the way we apprehend things. Not only does it cut physical activity, but it filters and inhibits sensory stimuli. We do not touch, see, and smell the way we did. Has this changed the way we interpret the world? It might be a good subject for researchers, the same sort of scientists as the ones I read about recently who were putting kittens into a room where they only had horizontal stripes before their eyes. When they grew up into big cats, they could not recognize vertical stripes, these were not part of their store of references. What are the references of the car children? Are they blind, perhaps, to everything that moves at less than forty miles per hour?

What have they lost forever from the reference libraries in their heads? Go to it, researchers, but hurry, you may not even have any controls left as it is.

This is the sort of work that could be carried out by a family or a team of scientists, working from one generation to the next. Father and son could follow the car children from the carriage to the hearse. Then perhaps they could catch that subtle moment when the addition of horsepower turns into a subtraction of strength, when Phoebus' chariot burns out and falls to earth as the wheelchair. Youth can stand anything . . . cars, cigarettes, education, the perpetual jet lag of its biological clock brought on by night living with artificial light (which has not been around much longer than cars as far as the ancestors of most of us were concerned). Then a discontinuity seems to appear. We do not have a smooth transition from youth through maturity. Instead, youth is lost, all is lost, it is a reverse moult, the butterfly becomes a caterpillar. Lewis Mumford talks about somewhat the same process when he describes how we now discard old technologies, the ways of the past, instead of building and improving on them as our ancestors did. We are obliged to drop our youth like a beautiful shell, to leave it to the next generation to don and display, while we crawl defenseless towards some sort of security. By the time we realize what has happened, it is too late. We have been moved down the production line, we are the senior citizens, we are the pro-pension lobby. Fear appears; if we lose our security, we will lose our cars and our energy, we will be cut down from two hundred and fifty horsepower to one manpower. So we do not take chances, as we grow older, we prefer not to gain so that we need not venture. The car gives us that illusory freedom to move but, in fact, it is the cars that are free to move. Socially, we are bound, just as we are belted into the car; we cannot move for fear that we will lose our parking place. In the end, the car serves as a school for discipline when it is used in large numbers. It is a training ground for sheep. Anyone who accepts a traffic jam will accept anything.

And yet, in all this dullness, there is that imminence of death at best or, at worst, disfigurement and maiming. We accept this as part of our transportation system run by incompetent amateurs, that is, ourselves. As usual, the French seem to have outdone most other people in this respect. It is just about impossible to get a French driver's license unless one is "presented" by a driving school. So the future driver must take lessons at five dollars an hour, which can be five times what he himself makes an hour. The winner is the driver who gets his license with as few lessons, as little experience, as possible. One is worried sick if a friend or a relative is a few hours overdue on the highway in France, one has any number of acquaintances with bashed-in foreheads, glass eyes, rebuilt noses.

There is tension in the air of Paris, any intersection can deal a mortal blow. The driver is allowed to continue when the light turns orange if he is going too fast to stop . . . and there are ways of making sure of that. On a warm evening with the windows open, sleep may come to me softly until it is frightened off by the usual sequence of tires screeching, steel buckling, glass tinkling, a woman moaning, all for no reason at all, a trip to the movies, a visit to the children in the suburbs (those suburbs that would not exist, either, if the car had not destroyed the villages of Paris).

I think the tension must exist everywhere, even in well-behaved American cities. There is always the subconscious attention that must be exerted, all the good driving habits that must be practiced. No matter how you slice it, you are still flesh and blood shooting along at the speed of an eagle, only you have no feathers to slow the landing impact, you are not the master of your element, you do not have two-hundred-fifty-horsepower reflexes.

What I am getting at is that you can survive as a city-suburb driver but only at a price. You are under tension, you use tension, a synonym for force and strength. Use it up driving and you have less to use somewhere else. Tension is creativity; God knows how many Sainte-Chapelles of stained-glass windows are lost to Paris in its daily jousts with danger.

No one has a choice, everyone must play, the pedestrian and the bus driver, the cyclist and the aging Don Juan with his monkey glands by Austin Healey. The car takes it off the top, it skims the cream from the city, the Parisian does not have much left by the time he has reached safety. Nor does anyone in any big city. He is in a state of constant battle fatigue, he gets only a few weeks a year away from the front; we gave our combat soldiers better treatment than that.

I am talking about a loss of creativity at any level, not necessarily the work of art. I mean good building, good cabinetmaking, good shoemaking, good cooking, the kind of creating that comes from the human mind and hands working in a place that does not intrude upon one's substance, that does not pluck and jangle nerves just when they have been turned to the proper pitch for making music, for making anything. The city dweller uses sedation and stimulation to try to achieve this pitch as he fights off the assault of the car on his ears, his eyes, his nose, and his very life. Or he flees to the seaside and the countryside where, precisely in the very places where nothing at all can be done, he feels capable of doing anything.

Chapter 3

INTERSTITIAL LIVING

The automobile takes fifty-five thousand lives a year in the United States alone. How much life does the bicycle give every year everywhere? I do not know, there are no statistics, I can only judge from my own experiences.

Follow the rivers, follow the water. Up the Hudson in Manhattan, you can take Riverside Drive, use the foothpath, it is empty. Watch for the squirrels, they scurry up and over the wall separating the foot-path from the derelict park. Roll past Grant's Tomb; I once met a girl there, I hadn't seen her in twenty-five years. She was coming in from Scarsdale in a station wagon big enough to be barred from a no-trucking zone. I was riding up from Herald Square on a bicycle in the rain. I had bought what was damn near a diving suit for the trip, it made no difference. The rain squashed down my back and into my shoes. We met on the steps of Grant's Tomb and we sat for an hour in a student cafeteria on Broadway with our pasts while I fed quarters into a parking meter that was

mounting guard on the station wagon with my bicycle locked inside.

Roll past Grant's Tomb, past the Clare-mont Inn and the 125th Street dock of the Hudson River Day Line, past all that is gone, on and up Riverside Drive, over the George Washington Bridge and come out on the Palisades. There is a colony of rabbits on the New Jersey end of the George Washington Bridge. They are wait-ing there, biding their time, waiting to move into New York.

At the end of the bridge, turn right, hang onto the brakes, let 'em squeal, let the wheels go, down you go down the side of the Palisades, the human fly on wheels, and you are on the shores of the broad Hudson, a mile of sun and scum between you and the heights of Manhattan. There is a road along the river, the trees arch over it in summer, it is as civilized as any *gemütlich* lane in Europe. A sign says cycling is forbidden; pay no attention to it, the police don't. Just roll along the river, go up the river as Henry Hudson did. Don't knock New York, don't kick America; the city is dead, the country has gone to hell, but I don't know another city that size with a state park on the other side of its doorstep, mile after mile of wilderness and rabbits and heaven knows what else. You can take the bike about seven miles up, almost to Alpine. On the way you come across a house that witnessed the Revolutionary War, then the road ends at a marina with wire fences guarding the yachts from river pirates, protecting them from everything except the Hudson swilling at their sides.

I have never gone any farther north, I do not know what lies beyond. I leave it to others to discover.

There are discoveries to be made; these are new trails, they can hardly be discerned on the maps issued by gasoline stations that mostly indicate roads where gasoline can be burned and bought. There might be a way all the way up to Bear Mountain, I don't know, I leave it to Henry Hudson to find it, Hudson on a bicycle like La Salle; Hudson and La Salle, no wonder those river names did not last on automobiles.

For a cyclist the Hudson is a fresh airway into the wilderness. The city's other waterways are too busy working for a living to worry about what they look like. The East River takes on some airs along Franklin D. Roosevelt Drive but loses them pretty quickly around 96th Street. A pedestrian walk starts there; it is a good place to cycle, you won't bother anybody. No one has seen a pedestrian for years along the East River, where they are as rare as fish in the river. Perhaps there is a correlation with the introduction of chlorinated hydrocarbons into the environment (DDT, if you prefer, but scientists like to say chlorinated hydrocarbons, it sounds like a soft drink).

The pedestrian walk leads to a footbridge over to Randall's Island, one of the most deserted places in New York (where *The French Connection* hid out its heroin ring). The view of the city downtown is well worth the journey, traumatic though it may be. One day, I pedaled along the walk until I got to the footbridge, I walked up a spiral ramp, then wrestled the bike up some steps to the bridge. It is a lift bridge, it could be hoisted out of the way in case a big ship came up the river, perhaps a de-mothballed *United States* making a profit at last by hauling tourists around Manhattan Island, the latest addition to the Circle Line fleet; 5,000 passengers at $5 a head, the ship could make a trip an hour running at 40 knots, it would be a license to print money. Nobody would see anything, the whole waterfront would have to be rebuilt to solve the problems of loading and unloading, but people put up with worse to ride airplanes where they see even less.

On the Randall's Island side of the footbridge, a track laid out as an idyllic path ran past broken park benches set on the water's edge, right to the foot of one tower of the Triborough Bridge. It was somewhat eerie, riding there after reading what the papers say about crime in New York. Randall's Island is a lonely place, any lurker could have cut me down without a trace, with no one to hear my screams, just the East River stinking by, waiting like a foul-mouthed hyena to gobble up the corpse, to dissolve me as if I had been dropped into battery acid.

But there were no lurkers, Randall's Island runs right off the danger scale. Jane Jacobs has observed that neighborhoods become risky as they empty out. People in the street police the street. When the little stores close to be replaced by supermarkets, there are no more shopkeepers outside standing watch for customers and, indirectly, for crime. There are only the closed-circuit TV cameras of the supermarkets. Unlike the shopkeepers, they do not keep an eye on the street outside as well as on the stock inside. But if you empty the streets of all targets, of all signs of life, then the predators leave for want of prey. That was the case of Randall's Island. I could not imagine a lurker waiting for a venturesome cyclist, loitering there for weeks, months, or years, living on garbage thrown overboard from passing tugs, growing a knee-length beard and, in final desperation, hoisting a signal of distress in the hope that drivers might see it from the Triborough Bridge.

Lovers of wild life overlook Randall's Island and they are wrong. I have never seen bigger or wilder rats in my life than the ones that share the island with its other inhabitants, the patients of a mental hospital. The hospital is fenced off from the idyllic park but I once saw the other side. I had ridden over from Queens on the footpath of the Triborough Bridge and, losing altitude, I landed inside the hospital grounds on Randall's Island. I asked a nurse how to get to the Manhattan footbridge. She advised me strongly against going outside the fence, there was worse than rats there. Yet I had no choice, either I would get to that bridge or I would wander about the hospital grounds as dazed as the other shapes I could see on the island. I found a hole in the fence, I got through, I got the bike through, I almost patted the rats, I was that glad to see them.

Otherwise, the East River is not very frightening. There is the park around the mayor's Gracie Mansion and a hanging promenade over the motor highway leading south. In the 80s and the 90s, there are still two- and three-story houses off the river; there is Yorkville putting up a wall of ethnic identity against nonentity, it succeeds almost as well as Chinatown does.

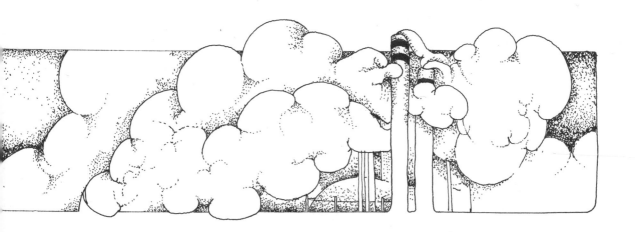

Not quite, though; it is just a little too paunchy from all that wurst and beer. I prefer my East River below 14th Street, that is where I prefer my New York. The bicycle has guided me to all the beautiful cities of Manhattan; the frame houses of Grove Court to the west, the Oriental columns and the pastel walls of the East Village, the inner turnings of Mercer and Greene Streets, Mott and Mulberry. It takes me to places I had never heard of on my native island, Republican Alley and Old Slip. Get there fast while they last, they're coming down.

Brooklyn Bridge isn't falling down, it carries automobiles, it is allowed to stay up. They zoom at your feet when you go over the bridge on the plank path shared by pedestrians and cyclists. I once crossed it in a winter dawn; I have never seen anything like it anywhere, red-pink light like stained glass inside the Gothic arches of Roebling's towers, those stone spires stuck in the bottom of the East River and put to work holding up a bridge. I was caught inside the spun web of the cables. Upstream lay Manhattan Bridge against the reddish-pink light, upstream from Manhattan Bridge the power plants were pouring out great clouds of white steam condensing in the cold, they were puffing away at full steam, the last of the tall-stackers, trying to keep Manhattan Island where it is, trying to hold it in the mainstream.

On the other side of the bridge, Jehovah's Witnesses give you the time and the temperature. If they weren't so pious, you would accuse them of lying when they flash 5° at you. It can't be *that* cold. Yes, it is, the heat that you had stored up overnight is running out, mittens can save your hands

but there is nothing you can do about your feet. You are like those European electric radiators that accumulate heat at night on the cheap rates, then trickle it out unplugged all day long. On Brooklyn Bridge, all the heat runs out all at once. You can hardly make it back to City Hall, then over to the diner on Canal Street that stays open every day of the year, New Year's Day included. A glass of tea will warm your hands before it warms your stomach, thereby warming your feet, tingling them back to life for a few more minutes, a few more miles until you are home.

Brooklyn Bridge leads to a number of places. There is bucolic Brooklyn Heights on the other side with the other view of Manhattan, this time with the castles and the cathedrals flattened to a silhouette against the curtain of the World Trade Center. From Brooklyn Heights, the port of New York becomes visible again. Freighters load at the foot of the Heights; it would be a good place to stroll or roll if it were not for the infernal six-lane highway plastered against the cliff of the Heights, three lanes at a time. I seldom cross to Brooklyn Heights, I keep it in reserve for the future. Instead I concentrate on the Manhattan side of the bridge, Fulton Fish Market down below, first the aerial view from the bridge roadway, then the market itself at six o'clock in the morning. Around Christmas is a good time to catch the market. The big porters climb up to the tops of open tank trucks to net eels for the Italian and Portuguese trade, the fish-crate fires roar around the pillars of the elevated highway that keeps drivers off the street and keeps the street away from drivers so they can never see it. They do not even know of the existence of Fulton Fish Market, Les Halles and Covent Garden all wrapped up and packaged at their doorstep, they cannot see it, they can only flee it. I push the bike through the market, I warm my rear on a fish-crate fire, a Jewish porter starts a conversation with me. Handcarting fish around the Fulton Market was one of the old trades of the Lower East Side. It is going; when the market is gone, it will be gone. No need to replace the old iron-rimmed carts, they're good for a few more years. You can see some that Stieglitz must have seen with his camera. They are almost big enough to be pulled by a horse, they are still towed by a man over the cobblestones of Front Street.

When the market is gone, the Seaport Museum will take over on Front Street. I like the museum, but it will not be the same. One must be thankful for small blessings, the museum pier is always open. At any hour of the morning, the cyclist can find a snug harbor of silence there after watching helicopters arrive with their high-priced cargoes of commuters to Lower Manhattan, so much more upper than the Lower East Side. On the museum pier, a cyclist can circle slowly in front of a schooner or a square-rigger or the Ambrose Lightship. At lunchtime, he can eat there, too, without worrying about someone walking off with the bicycle, there is a bike-in counter on the pier. Congress has devalued the dollar, but not bicycles. I don't know how much they are worth in New York. I once took one into a shop, I left it in a corner, a salesman told me: "Don't leave it there, it'll grow fcct." In Central Park on a Sunday, I saw a racer take his bike into the comfort station with him. I expressed

amazement, he knew better; the bike was worth four hundred dollars and he had already lost two outside that comfort station.

There is another pier where a ship sleeps on the Hudson River, a freighter used as a school by the city of New York. The ship's flanks catch the setting sun the way that the towers downtown reach for the sunrise. From the pier, you can see a retired Staten Island ferry. Manhattan seems to rest on its waterfront, where it once worked so hard. The ferry slumbers on the Hudson River, the police in their prowl cars pull up on the walks of the small stretch of park along the East River near the Williamsburg Bridge, sleeping the sleep of the just. The cops bat a sleepy eye when asked for directions, then they go back to their napping. No one is worried by a cyclist. People whose life it is to take the joy out of other lives do not go around on bicycles, such people are too important for that. So the bike is accepted everywhere.

It is even more adept at making friends if the rider happens to be a photographer with a French accent and a fascination for fire engines. In New York, the fire engines are like the private garbage trucks, they are great powerful tools, monuments to the high-priced American workingman. They go through the streets like an emperor; no dignitary visiting Paris in a puny Citroën with a motorcycle escort can flatten the city like a Manhattan fire engine. We once caught one down around Houston Street. The crew had stopped to inspect a theater. Two firemen were riding on the back platform; one looked as if he were on a seven-day bat. He had been out on twelve calls on a Saturday night in midwinter.

Fatigue slurred his voice and blurred his eyes, he had not shaved in two days. He was glad to see the photographer from France. "You're from France? Why, my mother was a hooker on the Champs-Élysées. She worked the right side." He looked at his buddy. "His mother worked the left side." His buddy looked at us. "You know how it is, there's one in every outfit."

We stood in the cold, talking to the firemen who stayed with their engine to prevent a frustrated bicycle thief from making off with it while the rest of the crew inspected the theater. It didn't take long, just time enough for me to botch a picture of the photographer wearing the fireman's hat. Then the driver came out, they all got aboard, the engine shrieked, and off they went, back into the pages of Currier and Ives: THE AMERICAN FIREMAN—*Always Ready*.

It was in Washington that we made the greatest haul of all these American urban fishing trips. We were in the streets of Georgetown, feasting our eyes and stuffing them on downtown frame houses and trees. A garbage truck came along the street, as it does sooner or later on every street. The cyclist becomes a connoisseur of garbagemen; they must necessarily go through the city more slowly than he does, he has ample time to study them. There are the garbage trucks of Paris with their Africans and Arabs on the back end and the European driver, reading his paper at the wheel. There are the monsters of New York that wrench ten tons at a time off the street. There is the farm tractor hauling a wagon that comes around every other Saturday in Lanloup in Brittany and inevitably stalls in front of the Duvals' café. But I have never seen anything like those Georgetown garbagemen. They belonged in the Olympics; no pro football team could have put on a better passing performance even with presidential play-making. Three men in orange worked the street. They sent great plastic garbage cans arching through the blue sky in mortar trajectories that landed them right into the basket on the rear of the truck. Then back went the cans to the owners' stoops in a series of flat lateral passes. One man on that crew was memorable, he was strong as a lion, graceful as a panther. His secret was the follow-through, you could tell by watching him. The garbage cans flew after the truck with his hands still fanned in their direction, driving them on in their flight with the field of force emanating from his fingers. He wasted no time with the photographer, the truck kept moving, so did he, so did she. She loaded and reloaded, focusing and clicking away at him while those trash cans floated through the air with the greatest of ease. There is nothing demeaning about street cleaning, not when it is a game of skill and strength like polo that only a few can play.

It was our bicycles that caught the Georgetown Redskins at practice; nothing can be hidden from the bicycle in a city. It brought me into the courtyards of Paris, even the one next to my own home where twenty years went by before I found Ossip Zadkin's sculptures tended by his widow in the garden of their house. The bicycle took me to the remote arrondissements of Paris where nothing of note ever happens, where the human species will survive a few more years until concrete overruns its sanctuaries.

I have come to think of the streets of Paris as the oceans that bound a continent. Travel along their shores and you will know the coastline. To know the continent, you must ride the rivers into its innermost fastnesses. So it is with courtyards. Through doorways, one enters another city of town houses and greenery, cobbled lanes and weathered shanties; one, two, three courtyards behind the street, the third level of consciousness. There in the soul of the city are sculptors and upholsterers, locksmiths and printers, the crafts and arts that need bulky equipment and plenty of space. There are fountains and gardens, vegetable farms and châteaux. There are old streets cut off by the façade of a new building on the avenue but running back, back, back into the innards of the block where you can turn around and see that the old street crosses the new avenue and keeps going through the newer buildings on the other side. The courtyards of Paris, I like to think, are its subconscious, where everything is deposited, where all is preserved until the New Parisian comes along with his bulldozers and his hollow bricks to house Eliot's hollow men in co-op coops for battery humans, wiping out all the layers of consciousness, lobotomizing the city, separating it from its memory.

In the courtyards, I found the city that Elliot Paul wrote about in *The Last Time I Saw Paris,* but not where he found it. His Rue de la Huchette no longer exists as he saw it. The buildings are still there but they might be in Disneyland, Florida; Mystic, Connecticut; Williamsburg, Virginia. The character is gone, it is replaced by characters, the rich who expensively dress poor, acting out a play that is all the more Living Theater because they do not even know they are actors themselves. Rue de la Huchette has gone through the travail that transforms urban villages everywhere into Greenwich Villages. It would be more honest to tear them down and put glass and ferro-concrete in their stead rather than leave this stage set, freshly painted in trompe l'oeil to look down-and-out, with its smellovision show of stale fat frying in cheap restaurants where the food is dreadful because it is cheap, thereby punishing all the New Parisians, tourists in their own country, who dare sin by stinting on their sacrifices. Adventurers from the far reaches of Auteuil and Westchester rub shoulders in the dives of Rue de la Huchette, providing local color for each other.

I prefer my courtyards where the last time I saw Paris it had not changed a whit since the next-to-the-last time. These are the recesses where humanity holes up, where a way of life survives around a tree, flowerpots at a window, ivy tumbling down the wall. Every courtyard dweller thinks he has a piece of the country to himself in the midst of the infested city. Each thinks his situation is unique because, obviously, he seldom goes out. He need not, he has a full feast for his eyes and his soul. Like the wandering tinkers who once brought the news from one lonely farm to another, I move from courtyard to courtyard on my bicycle. I keep an eye on the stone brow of the city for a new friendly wrinkle that gives away another principality in hiding.

Paris is like Gruyère cheese, more holes than solid matter, almost a Potemkin city that pretends to be a metropolis on its outward side but actually lives as a network of atoms interlinked as in those big molecular models used to teach chemistry. When I began to hunt courtyards, I would pedal off, coast along looking for a doorway, enter when one looked promising, spot some trees on the other side of a wall, wheel around the block, try to get at the trees, climb a flight of stairs for an aerial view, mumble to a concierge that I must have been at the wrong address, brave a dog that suddenly became fierce as soon as it could yap from its own doorway, forget where I was.

At first, I knew only a few courtyards. I was like their inhabitants, I thought them unique. One was behind the city hall near Les Halles. It was a rough lane, cobblestoned, with two bellying medieval buildings arched over it, forming a passage festooned with gas pipes and electric cables. Down at the end, daylight showed where a friend of mine was living in an old stable he had turned into a duplex. The ceilings were low but the house was quite liveable if one went around on all fours. He had been told that the courtyard outside had once been the Court of Miracles where the lame beggars walked and the blind saw in *The Hunchback of Notre Dame,* making the place at least as ancient as Victor Hugo. So began my Miracle of the Courtyards.

The next one I found started with another cobblestoned lane not far from Rue Mouffetard, la Mouff', that street of market stalls, Arabs selling lemons one by one, fruit stands decorated like a feast-day altar in front of the Church of Saint Médard. La Mouff' is dying, slowly choked by the necrosis that seeps down from Place de la Contrescarpe where the cheesy greasy restaurants are taking over along with the pubs imported lock, stock, and Watney's

barrel from Olde Englande. An Armenian shoe dealer who sells everything from espadrilles to sabots told me how it worked. A hole-in-the-wall business becomes an antique shop, an art gallery, a bar, all of them busy only in the late afternoon and at night. So, during the day, the street loses people. Shops trying to sell something useful find themselves high and dry, cut off from the sea of humanity in which they once thrived like fish.

I walked into the doorway not far from Rue Mouffetard. It looked promising, a high wooden double gate, a stone placed there as a convenience for those alighting from a horse, I imagine, and the rugged paving stones that have never been changed in these courtyards because they never wear out. Beyond the gates of the buildings, the hidden streets of Paris are paved as they were when Ben Franklin walked the city with that fresh all-embracing curiosity of his. Paris is not foreign to me in its old parts, it has more of my past as an American than many an American city where no era tails beyond its end, where every decade apparently has an automatic self-destruct button, timed to explode like a delayed-action mine—its artifacts, its traces on earth thrown away, destroyed like ten years of calendar pages. I go over the city of Paris again and again on my wheels, stopping, prying; each time I ride over it is like another chisel stroke in a woodcut. There is always room for another line, another miniature image in the great mural of a city that I am putting together in my mind.

I rode into the lane running off Rue du Cardinal Lemoine that leads into Place de la Contrescarpe. Beyond the gate, a row of two-story buildings. An illusion of an inner street, not a bad bag for the courtyard hunter. A tall, full plane tree at the end of the street. I ventured up to it. Always go to the end of the courtyard, it may not be the end. To the right, there may be a gap, a winding around a corner and into another corner, even more of a lull in the storm of a city. This courtyard did not end at the plane tree, nor did it wind. It opened into a blossom of lawn and lilac bushes bounded by two old town houses glorious in crumbling stone, flaking paint, shutters askew.

The place, so a sign said, was a *pension de famille*. Several times, I went into it, where I could smell the odor of measured portions and old lives running down as they, too, were measured to the last drop. I found no one there until, one day, a glum woman told me the building was coming down to make room for *studios* (a Paris *studio,* like a New York studio, is a large room that has been converted into a small room with bath and kitchen so that it can get a large rent).

I took the photographer, who is also a painter, to look at the courtyard during its last days, in that pause when old buildings are left alone, locked and barred with their memories, shut up to shut out the bums, before the bulldozers move in to knock down the ceilings and the floors, leaving only a faint imprint, a painted panel, a few bathroom-wall tiles, the pattern of a staircase on an adjoining wall. As we stood in the yard with our bikes, a little boy walked up, took a lilac from a bush, and went off into the street.

His mother emerged from the house. She was as slender as he was, she had the same open look on her face, she might have been her child projected against a screen so as to give a somewhat larger image. We talked to her; she and her husband had bought the *pension de famille* and they were going to make a small hotel out of it. Mainly, they wanted a place to live, a base from which they could send their two little boys out from a country house off Rue du Cardinal Lemoine to go to school with lilacs for their teacher. Nothing else would change, there would be no *studios,* the tattered carpet on the stairs would stay, so would the old corner room with both windows opening full into the embrace of the boughs of the big plane tree I had seen from the street.

Only the dining room would go, there would be no more old gray heads bowed as if in meditation over soup of leeks, wrapped in concentration while teeth, seldom their own, chomped bread and skinny skeiny beef, scraping clean the sides of little glass bowls to get the last cool acid drop of yogurt from them. The dining room did go, but the smells of that cooking lingered on for weeks.

They were not unpleasant, they talked to the painter as she worked in that corner room embraced by the tree. They talked to her in the intervals when she was left alone by the owners' two small sons who crept upstairs like mice, slithered into her room like snakes, then worked like beavers over the paper, paints, and crayons she dispensed to keep them busy while she went about her business. She worked well in her courtyard; whenever she had enough she charged down the stairs, ran over the grass with her big feet kicking high like a sprinter's, ran out the double gate on Rue du Cardinal Lemoine to a bakery for a loaf of bread, to a café for two cups of coffee boiling hot. She could have ordered a large coffee but then the second half would not have been as hot as the first.

I used the courtyard myself as an advance camp for my exploration of the twistings and writhings of Paris-off-the-street. I would return with my tales, my addresses jotted in a shirt pocket–sized notebook; I passed my scout's reports to the painter. Then, converted into a photographer, she sallied forth, camera on her back, lens case on her hip, the two of us awheel as we set out to record another image of the countryside-in-Paris, the city of gardens and children and old women that is going down faster than I can write it up, faster than she can put it onto film. That city is still so much bigger than the mites who are destroying it. It will outlast them, I think and I hope; I think and I hope that it will last as long as the two of us, that I will always be able to offer the photographer a new castle, a new bosk that she has not yet seen, a new cranny of the Paris that both of us had once crissed, crossed so unseeingly. I think it will last; I can discover five courtyards in one afternoon, she can take five afternoons to photograph one courtyard.

Once, she entered the life of an old lady on the verge of eviction from the country house she had occupied in the 13th arrondissement for fifty years. The old lady brought up her family and grew her vegetables there all within sight of the elevated Métro line that ducks in and out of the ground like a demented mole as it rings the inner city. When we met her, she was gathering her things together, her meek meager belongings, to make the move to a studio apartment in a high-rise that had been rented for her by her family. It was not that she disliked the idea of moving, she simply could not imagine it. She had no idea of what life is like in the city of Paris if one does not have a house, a tomato patch, a few hens for fresh eggs and, as neighbors, old workmen who come by every day to tend their allotments, turning over the soil, planting vegetables, pruning fruit trees, eating cherries off the branch, all within sight of the Métro.

The old lady used to have many neighbors. The wasteland around her had once been a city of coopers making the big barrels for the Halle aux Vins, the Left Bank wine market that has also died, its site marked by a tombstone of the usual glass, steel, and concrete into which science students have been funneled. I visited that wine market many years before, it wasn't a bad place in those days. There was one small building on stilts for the science students while tank cars full of Beaujolais and Big Red were switched between its legs. I had to do a story on the leading Paris dealer in Beaujolais. Next to the big clean vats in his market shed, I traveled through the litany of villages that make up Beaujolais, saying my beads with him: Saint-Amour, Moulin-à-Vent, Juliénas, Brouilly. The leader spat out the wine we tasted, I didn't. I had to write the story from memory, my notes were deep purple. I walked through the market into the dark cellars where I met an old man bottling his own brand of wine, sticking labels on by hand, truly an anachronism in his comfortable sweet-smelling cellar room under the high vaults that had been built in the days of the first Napoleon. The old man knew he had to go, he did not mind for his own sake; he only thought that he and his kind were more of a help to humanity than (a wave in the direction of the science school's first building) the others with their atomic bomb.

When the wine market went, the city of the coopers was bound to follow. I discovered it only by accident, following my glances into side streets, back alleys, front yards. Nearly all of the coopers' village had been demolished by the time I found it. There were only the houses of the old woman and her family, lone hummocks in the steppe of dust and ruts and weed-grown walls around them. The old woman was eighty but she had the blue eyes of a child, a diaphanous skin that was almost luminous at times, and white hair that covered her fragile head like a delicate veil of thin silk. It was the hair that bothered her, she had just done it, she did not want to pose with a scarf on her head. The photographer agreed; she came back the next day without me but there was not enough light to photograph the old woman in the yard of her house. She went back to the house at least twice more before she was able to get her pictures. Occasionally, I joined her and we prowled in back of the old woman's house, eating a few fresh cherries from a tree that had been left to its own resources in the few weeks of life remaining to it.

Through the orchards and gardens of the 13th arrondissement we roamed until we were met by a powerfully built man and his German shepherd dog, even more powerfully built. He was the watchman; he had been keeping an eye on us from his perch in the attic of a deserted two-story house. We got along well with the watchman because we took him seriously. First intruders, we quickly became his guests. He gave us a conducted tour through a magnificent town house that was coming down in a few days in the name of urban renewal: winter garden, billiard room, butler's pantry with call board, bathrooms upstairs and down, fireplaces, parquet flooring, all to be fed to the wreckers. The watchman was taking care to see that none of this fell into the wrong hands. While we were there, we watched as he and the dog and a friend moved a great mirror that had once looked down from over the fireplace. They heaved it and they hauled it, backing and filling and tacking downstairs through entrances until they reached the watchman's command post in the deserted house that was coming more and more to resemble a warehouse.

The watchman talked readily. Most people do in the courtyards of Paris. They are not city people fearful of strangers and movement but villagers at home on their own turf, confident and therefore not defensive. He told us everything except his name. He was one of those leftovers from the fall of the French Empire: *l'Indochine* is gone and so is *l'Algérie*. There is not too much demand for easy-talking men who swim best in troubled waters. One often meets them as watchmen outside some of the treasures of Paris, where they display the alert wariness, latent strength, and social ease that go with their role as men of the world, professional pacifiers in retirement. They are left with their dogs and their lonely patrols, waiting for the Viet Minh or the *fellagas* or Abd-el-Krim to turn up in the 13th arrondissement within sight of the Métro.

This arrondissement is my despair; it is

here that rural Paris is getting hit the hardest. Since it borders on the Latin Quarter, it allows the promoters to boast that their concrete filing cabinets for carbon-copy humans are "Left Bank residences." I rush at the 13th arrondissement on my bicycle like a man who has been placed before a smörgasbord and told he has only five minutes to eat all he can. I tote the bike through streets that end in steps where, on top of one, I found a parked bicycle with wooden rims on its wheels, wooden mudguards over them. It must have been there for years and years, left perhaps when its front tire went flat during the exodus from Paris in 1940, overlooked by occupiers and liberators alike, moldering peacefully on top of the steps. No one would steal a bicycle with wooden wheels, not even in New York.

Two doors away from the bicycle, I sighted a house with a telltale bust outside in a wall niche, almost a sure sign of a fallen mansion. I entered, I saw tall doors that had once opened into a stable. An old lady came out, the concierge who had been there since 1910. The house had been a hunting lodge for King Henri IV, she told me, and there were rooms upstairs over the entrance where the king could enjoy a little variety in his game. There was also a country pump she had to show me; she pulled away a few flowerpots, pried loose some boards, and there in the wall was the old pump, its long iron handle rusted but recognizable. The old lady did not mind living in the king's hunting lodge now that she had electricity, but she had to wait until the end of the Second World War for that.

Burrowing through Paris, I came across another old woman in the 15th arrondissement who was lighting with gas. I asked her what she did for wicks. She said there was still a shop on Avenue Emile Zola that handled them but she did not know what she would do when they closed. The possibility that her landlord might electrify never crossed her mind. There was no reason why it should have, the building was doomed. It stood in the way of the Paris of the Year 2000 that is going up on this other Left Bank flank of the Latin Quarter, edging out factories, rooming houses for Arab factory hands, and more more more gardens, farmhouses, backyard woods.

It was in this disaster area that I wandered one morning, fleeing the dust and the monstrous mixer trucks. I ducked into alleys and lanes, I had no idea where I had landed. And I saw a blacksmith shoeing a donkey. He looked up in irritation when he saw he was being watched, because the animal was skittish, then he went on with his work. He had a leather apron tied around his waist and a leather sling around his neck. He placed the donkey's hoof in the sling. This left his hands free; he took some nails from a pocket in his apron and hammered them home. It was serious business, he had neither the time nor the inclination to chat. He was shoeing the donkeys and the ponies that trot out every day from that unpaved courtyard in the 15th arrondissement to the Luxembourg Gardens and the Champ-de-Mars, where they carry children, some in carts, some on their backs. A country boy leads the animals and reassures the city children, delighted but a little fearful in the presence of beasts almost as rare as the panda, as exotic as the platypus, almost as extinct as the dodo in their city.

I was once riding down Rue de Sèvres, a Left Bank artery in the vein of Carnaby Street, when I pulled up at a red light next to a panel truck with a donkey inside. The driver told me he sold sachets of lavender, bottles of lavender toilet water in the street from a big basket on the donkey's back. The donkey provided an authentic touch of Haute Provence, where the lavender grows. The light changed, the truck moved off slowly. The driver said he was looking for a place to park. I asked him why he did not use the new underground parking lot that had been gouged out below Boucicaut Square, leaving the square with a layer of pallid grass and puny trees trying to grow over the scene of the crime. Oh no, said the lavender-truck driver, the donkey didn't like to go under the ground, he balked in the darkness where the shoppers parked. He may have been a donkey, he was no ass.

Rue de Sèvres is a good street for courtyard shopping. I go down it at least once a day; it always changes, depending on which gates are open. Two lead to convents and church schools; this is a neighborhood of nunneries and residences for the clergy. When the gates open, it is like looking into a magic Easter egg, an image of flowerbeds, shaded lanes, sleepy provincial old church schools. But the gates seldom open and they do not work automatically when you push the bell button. That is a trick I often use: I see a promising gate, I ring the bell, the doors swing open, I glance inside, take some mental notes, drink in what I

can, then shut them softly. On Rue de Sèvres and at other Church properties, this will not do. There is always a little grille at the door where one must state one's business. In many Paris convents, it is hard to find someone willing to allow a photographer to photograph the gardens and the henhouses and the sagging verandas. Nuns are well-trained to pass the buck; the ultimate power of decision lies somewhere in the provinces, they tell you with uplifted eyes.

This limits my activities, because nuns control so much of Paris behind the walls; businesslike nuns who run neighborhood dispensaries; wing-hatted nuns who dispense handouts to bums shuffling respectfully up to the convent door, hobbling on canes, pushing three-wheeled baby carriages loaded with gleaned garbage; lithe nuns in sweatsuits who teach physical education; young Irish nuns who speak French to you with a brogue. They are the vestals of the old city of Paris; they watch their sanctuary being nibbled away as the Church sells off properties to the builders. Half a convent goes down so that apartments can go up. The other half stands next to it, the paint of inside rooms on outside walls, old dark walnut doors that now open onto thin air. Every time we cycle by, the photographer says she expects to see a nun walk out one of those doors and fly away on the wings of her hat.

Adjoining houses are the best places to spy on convents, so I have been told. One Peeping Tom watches nuns work their vegetable gardens in the 7th arrondissement and tries not to miss the moment of their daily recreation when they relax with a wild game of volleyball. He is not really a Peeping Tom, he designs grandfather-clock-sized pocket watches or arm's-length thermometers in a shack three courtyards behind Rue du Cherche-Midi that runs back to back to Rue de Sèvres, providing a long swatch of country in the busiest part of the Left Bank, a rural stretch between two traffic-occluded colons, Boulevard Raspail and Boulevard du Montparnasse. I like riding down Rue du Cherche-Midi; cars always use it to beat the jam on Boulevard Raspail, then they get caught behind a moving van standing still on an all-morning job and the street is mine.

On Rue du Cherche-Midi, there are those high old doorways, tall enough to let a carriage through with baggage on the roof, tall enough to let a horse rear, that give away the presence of a mansion in the old aristocratic quarters. From under such a doorway, so a plaque tells me, Rochambeau left to fight alongside the revolutionaries in America. Two courtyards behind, an upholsterer works at his trade in one of those slanty wooden sheds, all splinters and fire hazards, that creak happily behind the frosted façades of Paris. The upholsterer will talk to you; courtyard people talk to the infrequent passerby once you assure them you are there to admire their courtyard and not take it away from them. They can understand this, they bask in your admiration, they show you a secret fountain, a hidden tower, a sculptured pediment. It is a good rule on Rue du Cherche-Midi, Rue de Varenne, Rue de l'Université, Rue de Lille, Rue du Bac, Rue Barbet-de-Jouy to look behind the high doorways. Space opens beyond, a preface of paving stones leading to the steps of a

town house, to the half-timbered walls and low gables of a stable where a Rolls is groomed, or even a road that runs up to houses facing a wood, parents lying in hammocks rigged to trees, reading and relaxing, unaware of their kids climbing out the attic window, wooden swords in hand like d'Artagnan, teetering on the edge of the roof gutters, whispering to us on the other side of the wall where we watch silently, with complicity.

Courtyards are rife in these quarters of Paris where nobles built without a care for space, leaving an odd acre of English park below their windows, a wilderness that betrays its presence to the street outside only by the cool breath that comes from the doorway on a hot summer day. In the back streets of these quarters, Rue de Verneuil, Rue Saint-Dominique, Rue Cler, Rue de l'Exposition, Rue du Gros-Caillou, the tradesmen work in courtyards of their own, overlooking more wilderness planted in flowerpots, oil drums, old tires, anything that will keep soil in place on top of cement. On a small street off Rue de Sèvres, a lady has a parasol and a table in the garden behind the little hotel she runs; she sits at the table and writes poetry when the sun and her inspiration are out.

There is also much for the eye to rest on in the working-class parts of Paris where space was laid on lavishly because land values were low. There, the gardens run off bumpy private streets never paved for the motor age, some still with center gutters to take what used to come out of the houses. I know an apartment house with allotment gardens behind it, to each tenant his own garden below. Population densities are high in these streets, but so are amenities for the population. Houses can stretch back a block or so, hidden forever from whatever is happening on the big streets. These little streets are called *villas* or *cités;* many were built to provide the most modest possible housing for workmen and artisans who now enjoy air, trees, gardens, grass, solitude, the most royal of privileges in the city of Paris. In the heat of June or July, kids romp naked through the *cités* and dogs run unafraid.

The situation is gradually being righted; step by step, little by little, these pockets of sanity and humanity are being cleared away, houses knocked down as if they were of cards, trees uprooted so that the soil can sprout high-rise beanstalks. Or even worse, the walls stay up, the roofs stay on, but the insides are gutted, the intestines are torn out to make way for rich stuffing. Such is the urban plight of Paris; the rich can destroy a city far more thoroughly than the poor. They can turn it into a exurb with none of the inconveniences of commuting. The suburban trains and the Métro are the lot of the fugitives chased from the city core. The result is the same as Westport or La Jolla; work is banished, dirty hands are the sign of the pariah unless they belong to maid or plumber. On Sundays, holidays, in July and August, these inner suburbs look as if someone had spread the word the Russians were coming.

It is among the aristocrats and the artisans, Faubourg Saint-Germain and Faubourg Saint-Antoine, that life still edges out death in the courtyards that the bicycle enters and leaves without a trace of its passage. This could be a model of urban planning, a city polka-dotted by the countryside. This could be the Paris of the Year 2000, the Paris for eternity, but the up-and-coming and the here-and-now will have none of it. The doorways of Passy are twice as high as those of Faubourg Saint-Germain, a double-decker bus could get through with everyone standing up; the concierge's lodge is twice as humble, the promise is that of a Versailles or, at the very least, a Fontainebleau behind the gates.

So I go in and there is a frosted glass door at the other end of the entrance. Bad sign that, must be something to hide. Open the door, a yard that looks more like an inch; they used to call it an airshaft in Hell's Kitchen. A monotony of yellowish brick, cheaper than the hewn stone outside, a building whose tenants enjoy neither light nor air, just the address out front. Behind it, more of the same. Those that built here knew the value of a square meter, they did not waste a millimeter, they raised their vertical deserts for the cream of Paris, letting it rise to the top by elevator. In the morning, the desert Bedouins become nomads in their cars, clotting the streets, clogging the air, agreeing only that *le progrès* has made city life impossible.

Chapter 4

THE BUILT-IN BREAKDOWN

Our cities have become a-creative. Once, they could offer promiscuity and isolation in the proper proportions. Moise Kisling, one of the Montparnasse painters of the Twenties, lived across the street from my Paris address. He could wander to the Dôme on Carrefour Vavin, meet his friends, drink with the others of the generation that funneled into Paris all the way from Poland to Mississippi; then he only had to walk a few hundred feet to be back on the bywater of our street where he could work to his soul's content. Not any more, Moise, not any more; by the time you reach the Dôme these days you need a stiff drink just to get over the trauma of getting over Boulevard du Montparnasse. I don't think you could get much work done in that studio of yours, either, you'd be worried too much about paying for it. Studios in Montparnasse are not for artists any more, they make great places for displaying objects by artists. Only the truly creative people of our time can afford them, people like psychoanalysts and real-estate agents,

who can create money directly without going through any intermediate phases like canvas or stone.

So, Moise, I have to leave our street whenever I have any real work to do, anything that involves more than just going through the motions of work, more than repeating with but a slight variation what I had done the day or the year before. I have found a place in Brittany where it rains so often that the grass stays green all year long and the Parisians come only in July and August. You just keep going west from Montparnasse, out of the belt of wealthy suburbs that has its buckle on Saint Cloud bridge where the Autoroute de l'Ouest begins. You leave behind the Beverly Hills communes for film stars around Montfort-l'Amaury about twenty miles out, and after that the sailing is almost clear. Paris has smeared south towards Lyons and the Mediterranean; the high-speed trains run that way and so do the high-speed cars along the Autoroute du Sud. But going west towards Brittany, the Autoroute de l'Ouest peters out well before Montfort. There are forests and farms. When you go west by train, the country quickly becomes compartmented by hedgerows after the plains around Chartres. By automobile, the way can be almost as lonely, there are still roads that were used by the postriders and the stagecoaches. I take them to go to Lanloup on the Breton coast, where the words I have lost in Paris come back to me.

A few years ago, I might have gone to Lanloup by train. I could have taken an express to Saint-Brieuc, then the narrow-gauge branch line that ran down the coast. Brehec by the sea was a station for Lanloup a mile-and-a-half inland, the viaduct of the abandoned narrow-gauge line still stands there. It was built by giants, no doubt, the midgets who replaced them are not even up to the task of demolishing it. I might have come by the steam train that screamed on the viaduct like a gull over the cliffs, whistling with its two eaved passenger cars, a brake van, and two or three freight cars. I could have got off the train and taken a trap up the hill to the Duvals' café where I rent rooms right across the road from the Lanloup church. There I can work in the Seventies, it is the kind of place that my street in Montparnasse must have been for Kisling in the Twenties. I once arrived there on an Easter Sunday. I had to come by car because the bus that plies the corrugated roller-coaster track of a highway from Saint-Brieuc could not have carried my two bicycles. I wasted no time breaking out a bike and coasting down a road that runs from Lanloup to the sea through a valley carved out by the stream Kerguen. There were once seven mills on

that stream, only one is left and it grinds no more.

On the beach at Brehec, just on the downstream side of the railroad viaduct, there was a sheen of wet sand in the artificial cove formed by a breakwater built many years ago to protect fishing craft. Most of the fishermen are long gone. In winter, there is only one working boat left in Brehec harbor, the *Marcel Augustine,* named after the parents of the two catlike young men I see aboard when they moor in the middle of the cove and scull a dinghy to the foot of the breakwater with a few crates of scallops.

The cove was empty on that Easter Sunday morning, it was awaiting the play-boats of the summer yachtsmen and the dinghy sailors. Except for two or three cafés, nothing was open in Brehec. The summer houses were shuttered against a miraculous Easter Sunday sun that sent me walking shirtless across the wet sand. The hotels were battened down for the winter, their windows not only shuttered but blinded by sheets of fiberboard nailed over them. I sat on the beach; I had half an acre of sand around me to blot my ink, but the sun and a breeze from the West dried it as soon as I wrote, dried it as fast as a ballpoint. I got back up the hill, pedaling against the grade and the trickle of the Kerguen, just in time to see and hear the twin bells of the Lanloup church calling the village and the countryside around for high mass, their clappers lolling like tongues inside their cupped brazen mouths.

Except for July and August, one is high and dry in Lanloup, safe beyond the reach of urban sprawl. It was not easy to find Lanloup. Nearly every other place I sought had been tainted by the car city. Mere distance from downtown is not enough protection, the car people can sprout wings and flutter off to the Bahamas or the isle of Elba. I once did a piece of work in a village on the Seine near Fontainebleau. A hundred years ago, there was no one there except a few farmers and a boatyard where wooden river barges were built. During the Twenties, it saw an epidemic of great summer houses, it looked something like the North Shore of Long Island except for the modest moat of the Seine instead of the mighty Sound at the feet of the houses. Then, after the war, it went back to the pre-car era, not much was heard except the river barges hooting for the lock in the early-morning fog. But the tide kept spreading out from Paris; it swallowed up Corbeil down the river; on the other side of the city it puddled east to overwhelm the Marne valley; finally it reached the village where I had once been able to work. Old country inns were either sold off as apartments or refurbished with plate-glass doors and thatched roofs. The village was not

crowded, it was even emptier than it had been before, but I could not take my ease there any more. It was no longer a place to work; it will soon lose its identity, it has only a river and a rim of forest to protect it as a community from the car.

The car distorts communities just as it bloats and misshapes individuals. It literally deforms cities. I realized this a few years ago when I saw Leningrad for the first time. My eyes could not adjust to it, something was awry, it took me a while to realize what it was. For the first time in my life, I was looking at a classical city from head to foot. Leningrad was almost carless, it had not

been amputated below the knee; from roof to street, I could take it all in. Every other old city I know is washed over by the tin flood, their monuments stand on a mobile junkyard. The car erodes these cities, it gnaws away at their feet, it throttles their windpipes, it consumes them. It must feed on them to grow, it must grow to keep producing its rewards for those who make and fuel it. That is why the car cannot solve any urban or suburban transportation problem. It *is* the problem. It must inevitably lead to the discarding of cities, for they are frightful places to park cars. Inevitably, too, we must have the exodus to the suburbs, frightful places to park people, those consumer parks where productive work is taboo, where there is nothing to do but drive and buy.

The leapfrogging starts, the suburb becomes the city, more cars are needed to get away from it, more roads are needed to carry the cars. Another chunk of the rural landscape is bitten off, chewed, digested in the intestinal tract, spat out as tracts. There is a premium on change, there is money to be made in tearing down and building anew. It is the car that is the prime mover of change; we use it to go places, to go from the places that it has made unbearable. They are left behind to become slums, no, ghettos, a new word that implies no chance to escape, not a stepping stone but a tombstone. The old communities in the United States are being wiped out and the new ones aborted. In Europe, an urban tissue constructed cell by cell over millennia is being shredded in a few moments for a new race of courtiers who demand of their cities only convenient parking during the week and an easy exit on the weekends.

Industry goes along with the exodus. IBM forsakes New York for Westchester, American Can runs to Connecticut. According to Robert Cassidy, a city planner writing in the *New Republic,* St. Louis lost forty-three companies to the suburbs in 1970 and, in two years, Boston found that seventy-five had gone. These are all clean industries, of course. It is the headquarters that move out, the hindquarters are left in the old urban industrial holes. These are executives and secretaries, they are clean livers, the only thing dirty about them is the cars that they drive. Yet that should be enough, as I know from my acquaintance with Paris. A canary could hardly survive in those parts of the city where the only activity is shopping and looking for a place to park. I'm not much on wine but I'm a pretty good air-taster and it's hard not to inhale on a bike. The worst breathing in Paris is not around the industrial north and east anymore but in the plush west, that ghetto of the rich, the festering avenues that move the tin carriage trade through Passy and Auteuil. Greenwich and Larchmont, take note, there's more than just money moving up from New York, the muck is coming along with it.

Mass transit does not stand a chance when it is placed against this kind of competition. As someone has pointed out, it must buck the laws of geometry. The farther you move from the center of a circle, the farther you must travel along the periphery and in those interstices the automobile multiplies. The commuter railroads of the nineteenth century were responsible for the hatching of our urban dinosaurs but, at least, they gave the countryside a chance, offering breathing spaces between stations and farmland between lines. The car butters the goo evenly over the whole circle, a homogeneous layer that cannot be scooped up in big enough quantities to make public transit worthwhile.

The automobile was never intended for cities, it is self-defeating there. In limited numbers, it could offer quick, convenient house-to-house door-to-door movement of goods and services, perhaps as quick and convenient as our great-grandparents enjoyed with horse cars, hansom cabs, and brewery wagons. The mass car breaks down in the city because there is a built-in breakdown. It is like the clowns' cars that fly apart at the end of the circus act. We build more freeways for it when it runs out of roads, then we run out of air.

Yet that is the saving grace of the full-power wheelchair in its present form. The crud over our heads is the ceiling of our automobile population. Far worse would be the pollution of the nonpolluting car. Then we could sextuple-deck the Long Island Expressway, shuffle off to Buffalo at the end of a day at the new World Trade Center down at the already drained Battery . . . but this is just science fiction. You can't burn oil without polluting and when cars stop running on oil, there is a chance that oil will stop running us and we will stop living on energy borrowed from geological time with no intention of repayment.

Since this energy is not ours, we feel no need to conserve it, we throw it away. Perhaps the throwaway car was the start of throwaway living. Never before have goods of such importance lost their value so quickly. Perhaps it is because they destroy rather than create. Creative work does not depreciate, it appreciates all the more in our car time as it becomes more and more scarce.

It is in moon travel that one finds the fastest depreciation of all. This is the ultimate projection of the car-travel society. There is instant depreciation; the booster stages and the fuel vanish, only the capsule arrives (with the relative residual value that my '47 Chevy would have today). Perhaps we get into trouble when our tools, our goods, do not live as long as we do. A house does, a trolley car or a locomotive or a steamship used to be good for a generation or two. The car cannot last because, like the moonship, it consumes itself as it consumes energy.

Sooner or later, it consumes us, mentally as well as physically. The car bestows power without responsibility. The airline pilot, the steamer captain, the locomotive engineer control much more power, but their every move is governed by skills that take years to acquire and rules that fix responsibility in every foreseeable circumstance. Not we in our cars; we get the power for nothing, we pay insurance companies to take the rap, thereby giving them a swollen role in shaping our world. The car puts all of us on horseback; we can multiply our own speed and power as our predecessors could only by riding fleet horses, again almost a professional skill and certainly one that demands much more physical and psychological effort than guiding an automobile after a few hours of lessons.

So we are all men on horseback. In the United States, the man on horseback is the cowboy, a workingman in working clothes. His image has covered the world, he is imitated in *Les Corrals du Far West* on the banks of the Yonne or in dude ranches behind Mandelieu on the road to Cannes. His were the free and easy ways of Americans on horseback, they are transposed into the manners of the car driver in America. He gives the right of way to the weak, he stops to offer his help at a sign of trouble, it is the old fraternity of the cowboys on the plains. The Americans invented hitchhiking, a form of instant hospitality and generosity. Signs of such behavior are found throughout the United States, even in a city like New York. Scoffers (and I know there are many) are advised to try crossing a street or riding a bicycle in such cradles of civilization as Paris or Rome.

In mother Europe, the man on horseback has a different meaning. His power is political, he is a military man, Napoleon crossing the Alps, General Boulanger saving France from democracy, all the grand butchers of Europe's wars leading their pedestrians to slaughter. There is a social Grand Canyon between these horsemen and the muddy manure-spattered European cowherd whom no one would dream of emulating. Still, the nearest thing I ever saw to the Wild West on either side of the Atlantic was a farm boy in the upper Marne valley. He was driving the herd home and riding the last cow, holding her between his thighs, riding bareback, no reins, no hands. I was with my dear friend, the photographer, I wanted her to get a pic-

ture, but the light was falling fast, faster than we could cycle over to the pasture. The cowboy was cooperative; he rode his cow almost into the ground, but the exposure meter said no and we had no flash. It was just as well, that cow would have jumped over the moon with the boy on her back if we had focused lightning on her from the big black round eye that always sends the cows cowering. The cowboy told us he could ride only one cow in the herd, the others weren't used to him. He would be glad to ride a cow any time for the photographer if she came back to take his picture. He told her this in all sincerity, his eyes looking at her haunches the way he must have sized up the cow's before he took his flying leap to mount them for the journey home.

He was the king of that pasture of his, he stood over us on our bicycles, he commanded power just as the farmers do on their wagons hitched behind the heaving buttocks of a Percheron on the roads of Brittany. There are not many left, but it is a fine sight to see such a rig plodding along, the big horse in front, the man standing behind and, on the wagon bed, a calm German shepherd dog. Horses survive here and there on French farms. In 1970, I saw an elderly couple hitching theirs to a buggy outside the church in Honfleur after the market had closed. They only had three miles to go from their farm to the market; the children used to drive the truck to town but now they were grown and gone. The parents were too old to learn to drive, so they let the horse drive.

None of this interests the Parisian. His origins were in the provinces, he or his parents spent years losing their accents, changing their manners, forming and conforming. The cowherd is not his folk hero. When he drives a car, he does not identify with the peasant. He becomes a military man on horseback, he must swoop to Moscow, he is invincible at Austerlitz. Bottle him up in a traffic jam on Elba and he rides up from Cannes, rallying the country to his banner, averaging a hundred thirty-eight kilometers an hour all the way to Waterloo. The infantry is expendable, a whiff of grapeshot is all that is needed to scatter the mob, the unmounted rabble. He does not clean and water his horse; that is for the groom, the hostler, the mechanic, the rabble on foot. He has the double prestige of the horse and the carriage. The horse multiples his power, the carriage (in French, *voiture,* the same word whether the vehicle is driven by two horses or four cylinders) grants him isolation.

He does not come into contact with the street, his sedan shields him as the sedan chair once did. What is occurring in the city reaches him only through glass. Anything between his point of departure and his point of arrival is an obstacle that should be cleared from his path. Since one of the characteristics of the automobile is an infinite choice of itineraries, one man's goal must necessarily be another man's obstacle. The consequence is that great swatches of city and countryside are flattened. The tall plane trees that made travel in France a journey through a bower were removed from main roads because drivers kept running into them at eighty miles an hour. Instead of a speed limit, a tree limit was adopted. That ended a delightful transition era of motoring when the car had not yet murdered all that it touched. I admit, there

was an exhilaration about coming out of a mile of hot yellow wheat in August, then diving into the plane trees, the shade bathing the road between the trunks, the cool air massaging your face through the open windows. The early age of driving is like the early age of smoking: the pleasure is keen, one can do anything, one becomes hooked and so hopelessly that one cannot stop when the side effects start to catch up.

I keep talking about France because, in a way, this country has offered me the same living laboratory that the Veterans Administration hospital provided the scientists studying the relationship between smoking and cancer. While it pioneered the automobile, it did not experience the mass car during the Twenties and Thirties. It lay somewhere between the United States of the Tin Lizzy and the Soviet Union where film audiences gaped at *The Grapes of Wrath,* not because the poor Arkies and Okies were forced to move, but because they were able to move in cars. When I first came to France in 1944 and landed in Normandy, American jeeps and trucks were the only motor vehicles around except for a few cars that had been rerequisitioned by the Resistance after they had been liberated from the Gestapo. They ran on gas generated by burning wood in a big furnace carried outboard on a fender. We came with our militarized traffic jams and the French watched us in amazement.

When I returned in 1948, only surplus jeeps and trucks were left and French cars were so rare that they could be bought new only by paying for them in dollars which were even more rare (this was a LONG time ago). Paris was a city that could be taken in from a sidewalk café or from those rolling sidewalk cafés, the open platform buses that snorted through streets empty except for periodic demonstrations when Communists would pick up the street and throw it at the police in bits and pieces. The open platform buses are gone and it is too bad, they provided an interesting solution to the problem of serving territory between stops on a bus line. Parisians were athletic in those days, they caught their buses on the run, the crowd leaning over the platform and cheering them on, helping hands reaching out to bring the racing passenger into the fold. Or they got off in between gear changes while the conductor grumbled, *"Ce n'est pas l'arrêt,"* and turned his head. There are no more conductors, there are no more open platforms, the buses are hermetically sealed even between stops when they are stopped which is most of the time.

Parisians look back on this period with little nostalgia. They did not have to diet because they were rationed. They did not have to exercise because they ran for buses or cycled out to Nogent-sur-Marne on a Sunday, Monsieur and Madame on a tandem, the baby behind in a trailer. Cars were a curiosity, most of them had been up on blocks during the war and they appeared in public as gingerly as their proprietors, who preferred to gloss over what they had been doing during the war. It was considered bad form to have a new car unless one was American and in those days in Paris it was not considered bad form to be an American. The breed was encouraged; not only could they buy cars but they were given liberal gasoline rations to run them. The French had no rations at all, but they ran their cars just the same. Any Frenchman who had an American for a friend didn't need an oilwell.

Overnight parking was forbidden. This is probably the most effective way to keep the population of cars and lovers down in a city: a car for every garage, a garage for every car. But it was no way to sell cars. In no time at all, the overnight parking ban came off and the great race was on to keep Paris ahead of the automobile. Streets were widened, acres of sidewalk were whittled down to slats in order to gain two traffic lanes up to the next bottleneck where more trees had to come down and more curbs were forced to retreat. Or the sidewalks themselves were converted into parking lots, officially as on Avenue des Champs-Élysées, unofficially as on every other avenue.

The car became a religion in Paris, perhaps more so than anywhere else. The Parisians have the lowest standards of housing and the highest proportion of car ownership of any Western European city in their league. The old class lines that had blurred somewhat in the immediate postwar confusion were being etched in again . . . and the easiest way to get across a line was to drive across. Every Parisian could be a man on horseback, every man had the power to crush the infantry that got in his way. The tin armor of body panels and the visor of the windshield came between the Parisian and the city streets from whence he himself had sprung not so long ago. He was not sure of the title to his new nobility, he had to keep asserting it all the time. Just as the converted Jew is supposed to be the worst of anti-Semites, the postwar Parisian with a new car was merciless with the pedestrians who reminded him of his humble condition of only yesterday. He was hardly less harsh on his peers, the drivers who had the effrontery to get in the way of his daily trip to *gloire* and *grandeur*. The car became his identity, so much so that the French post office adopted the license-number code to designate postal address zones. A Parisian does not get his mail addressed to the Seine *département* any more, the envelope just says "-75-." The Breton in Lanloup is 22, the number that cars from the Côtes-du-Nord *département* carry. What more identification could you have with the car; these people live in their license plates.

The old European drive for living space has been sublimated into a push for parking space. The Parisians are becoming bolder. In 1939, they said they weren't going to die for Danzig, today they die for a place to park, screaming and fistfighting and kicking until one of the two adversaries is felled by his infarctus. Etiquette as rigid as the protocol at the court of Versailles governs these encounters on the streets of Paris. For refusing to grant the right of way, one is accused of being a homosexual's mistress. For taking the right of way, one is accused of being a female private part (the male private part is not used pejoratively in France as it is in English-speaking countries, a difference that could probably generate some fruitful psychoanalytical research). Using English on a Parisian driver is as unpardonable as trying to take the right of way on a bicycle. I do both. In extreme cases, I used to spit on cars but I stopped doing that the day a

Ford Capri spun around in a U-turn and headed straight at me. Then I knew how an antelope feels when it is hunted by a sportsman with a high-powered rifle in a low-flying plane. I also bang on roofs. This is pretty effective because, in most French cars, the driver already feels that he is riding around in a beer can and he expects the whole thing to collapse around his head at any minute.

New York muggers are far less dangerous than middle upper-class Parisians. In my own experience, I have found the streets of Paris to be much more reassuring during a riot when traffic is blocked than they are when domestic tranquility reigns and traffic keeps moving. Moving? Flying . . . strafing, roaring through the gears, tires scorching as the green light drops like the starter's checkered flag at Le Mans, through the gears up to fifty in a yellow-orange Renault R-8 (the same as the standard model except that it has four headlights in front and a big amplifier in back in the motor compartment, that's where they keep the cartridges—a flick of the finger and the driver can change the tape so that his engine stops snarling like a Jaguar and starts purring like a Ferrari . . . or he can shut it off so that it sounds like a Rolls Royce). And so one goes through gears and through life in Paris where the sidewalks are safe and the streets are lethal.

A really big traffic jam is a lifesaver. Such jams occur whenever more than ten percent of the drivers in Paris decide to use their cars at the same time. A Métro strike provides such an occasion, a three-day weekend another. The biggest jam, the jam with thirty-two flavors, the time that the streets of Paris were paved with solid steel, rubber, and evil intentions, came in June 1968, when the great gasoline strike was broken by General de Gaulle so as to put an end to the "events" of May. He used light mobile units against striking tank trucks as he was never able to use them against striking German tanks in 1940.

With the police guarding the garages— I don't know whether they were *gendarmes, Compagnies Républicaines de Sécurité, officiers de la paix, gardes champêtres, Sûreté Nationale* (France has as many varieties of cops as it has varieties of cheese, hence the expression: *"Fromage it, the gendarmes!"*) —the gasoline trucks got out to the thirsty pumps of Paris, long drained by long lines of Parisian drivers who had filled tanks, wine bottles, jerry cans, and bathtubs (for many, it was the first time they had used the bathtubs that came with the apartment they bought to have a fashionable address) in expectation of *la révolution, l'occupation, la collaboration,* and *la liberation.* As soon as the gasoline trucks began to roll, nothing else did. The trucks moved through town like freight trains with a long clanking of cars behind them. As soon as a tank truck began to pump gas into a service station, the cars began to take it out, filling up so that they would be able to get on the tail of another tank truck.

The ensuing jam lasted forever. Not only did some women have babies in stalled cars, but others had the time both to conceive their kids and deliver them. They never saw the fathers again after the jam was finally cleared, I don't know how, probably by lumberjacks flown in from *le Québec,* who worked the frozen rivers of steel from the tops of the cars with their peaveys, prying loose a Peugeot, tilting a Simca, logrolling a Cook's bus just for kicks.

To get away from all this, the Parisian acquires a country home or, to put it properly, he takes his city home to the country on weekends. In a way, this is worse than American suburban sprawl because it is more wasteful. The American has only one house and garden, the Parisian has his city apartment and then, leaping over the outer scab of high-rise suburbs, he has his *résidence secondaire.* There is supposedly one such residence in France for every thirty-two persons, compared to one in seventy-seven for the United States. The poor French farmer gets it both ways: the Parisian rigs the wheel so that the farmer is driven off the land into a job in the big city, then the Parisian moves out onto his farm. The barn becomes a duplex studio– living room, mullioned windows replace frank open panes, a big hole is torn out of the once-generous earth to plant an oil tank, the outhouse vanishes because it does not go with an in-house. Monsieur mows the lawn or, on rainy days, figures how much value his property has acquired since last Sunday. Madame gets fresh air and oxygen by driving down to the Hôtel du Coq d'Or in the village, where they have roasted her chicken for lunch.

The French themselves are worried. A report by the National Institute for Demographic Studies states: "As France has the privilege of having the most cars in Western Europe with the least amount of use per individual auto, we are about to have the greatest proportion of country homes at the same time as the highest overcrowding rate in our primary housing." Paris can also boast of the lowest ratio of parks to people of any comparable big city. The Parisians who matter have their private parks sixty miles away; a six-lane chunk is torn from a public park like the Bois de Boulogne to help them get there.

Parisians without country houses, according to legend, spend their weekends driving around on the outer boulevards, circling the city until late Sunday, an acceptable time to return home and open the shutters while the neighbors look on. Then there are those who cannot even afford an apartment with a good address in Paris, let alone a country house. They are in a predicament, *le standing* does not allow them to live in a dormitory suburb, *le budget* bars them from the big city. Thanks to the car, they have been able to get out of the city and stay in it. It is the car that has made Parly II possible.

Never heard of Parly II? Just mention the word when you hear a supercilious Parisian lecturing about the desert of American taste, the Sahara of our *savoir-vivre,* the Gobi of our billboards and our shopping centers. Say the magic words: "Parly II" and he will fall silent, probably for the first time in his life. Every day and in every way, Parly II is strengthening its claim to the title of the most retched place in Europe.

The name alone shames all rivals. When its creator first had the idea of putting up blocks of identical flats in the country— one design infinitely reproduced right out of the cookie cutter but the architect's fee is 8 percent so all he has to do is sit back and make sure nothing happens to his right hand that might prevent him from cashing checks—when *le promoteur,* as the real-

estate shark, the barracuda of the building game, is known in Paris, decided to get decay out of the city by moving it into a forest, he wanted to call his project Paris II.

It was a Eureka moment, that one, in the history of the earth-blight game. In his fertile brain, he saw concrete piling up alongside streets bearing the names of the most sought-after addresses in Paris. The mark would be able to move in and Madame Mark could get her stationery printed up: "The Marks, 1 Rue de la Paix, Paris II." No, better make that PARIS ii, get it down to agate, small enough so that it won't be noticed by anyone except the postman.

Like all other great ideas in France, this one went unappreciated. It was killed by small men of small vision. The Paris Municipal Council raised bloody hell, spurred no doubt by constituents living in places like 1 Rue de la Paix, Paris I. It was Verdun all over again. Nothing was sacred— burgundy grown in California, champagne in New York State, cognac in Armenia, the Americans had even stolen *la guerre d'Indochine,* and now someone was trying to make off with the good name of the capital itself. Paris had not raised that much hell since the Trojan Wars. It got its way, it liberated itself without the help of Hemingway. Paris became an *appellation contrôlée,* no other city in France had the right to use the name, it was proprietary, like Coke.

Since Paris II needed another hook for the sucker bait, it became Parly II. This combined the original name and that of nearby Marly-le-Roi, a town too feeble to protest, for it was still suffering from the amputation of SHAPE headquarters, the last square millimeter of French soil to be freed from foreign despoilers. Marly was also freed from a couple of thousand well-off families, thereby turning it into a disaster area for landlords and shop-keepers. It was too weak to defend its name. Settlers at Parly II could now answer the embarrassing question of what the name of the place had been before it was Parly II. The whole matter has been resolved and will probably stay that way until Paris decides to get a new image, to lure the exiles back by changing its name to Parly I.

One day, I wheeled into Parly II shortly before high noon on my piebald Peugeot bike. I climbed down from the saddle and looked for a place to hitch the bike. Not a post in sight, just a spiral ramp that led into the parking lot under the shopping center at Parly II, the biggest in all Europe. So I took the bike into the shopping center, one of the boys from the Big Bend country, afraid to go out in the city without his horse for company. The bike wheeled obediently with nothing more than a loose hand on its saddle to guide it. I saw no one else walking bikes through the shopping

center but it couldn't have harmed the marble floor any more than a shopping cart or a baby carriage.

On I walked, my head aswim. *Musaque,* I guess that is what they called it in Parly-sian, poured out of hidden speakers. It was an air terminal all over again without the airplanes. This was true progress, far ahead of the laggard Americans who build suburban shopping centers with parking lots for cars. Parly II has lashed them to the mast; it has built a parking lot for people, customers by the hundreds, by the thousands, glued out in their concrete flytraps somewhere between Versailles and the Autoroute de l'Ouest, nothing to see but more flytraps, no one to talk to but more trapped flies, nothing to do but shop, shop, shop all week long by themselves, then shop some more on Saturdays with the husbands and the kids.

This was a factory farm for consumers, no more free ranging through street markets, no more pushcarts, no more Maman-et-Papa shops, just the grand concourse of Parly II, the colors, the lights, the fountains, the palace of the new Versailles where every man is a sun king. And no

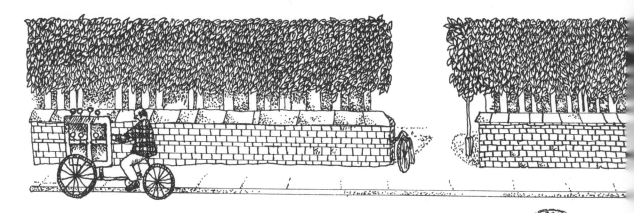

bistros, bars, cafés to speak of, just a little place for cigarettes and newspapers and a few tables, very few. Investments don't get amortized over a round of *pastis* or *vin blanc;* at the shopping center in Parly II, they keep 'em walking, there's no time for leisure in the *société des loisirs.*

There is less than an ocean between us and Parly II. Paris has always pioneered not in industrial innovation but in the invention of such new political forms as centralization, military dictatorship, the reign of terror, and, most recently, videocracy, government by monopoly TV. In the United States, the automobile is now giving us more spatial but less social mobility, a tendency to seek the same homogenizing social zoning that Paris has achieved. IBM doesn't set any precedents when it goes to Westchester, Louis XIV moved his whole operation to Versailles two hundred fifty years before.

Chapter 5

MAN THE MECHANICAL RABBIT

I had to come a long way to get to Parly II on that piebald Peugeot PX-10 with its Reynolds steel frame from England and its Campagnolo pedals from Italy (a Paris dealer once bragged to me that nothing was French on his best French racing bike except the clip that held the rider's water bottle). I had come a long way from my old black-wheeled horse with the rubber saddle painted to look like leather and the built-in swerve to starboard every time I let go of the handlebars. It was long gone, sold to a friend's son and stolen thereafter. I was sad to hear of its loss. On it I had ventured to work a dozen years before in my little black ensemble: bicycle, raincoat, briefcase, outlook on life, all matching. That is the start of cyclotherapy, the first timid step, when the bike is just a better way to get to places that one should never go to at all.

Many cyclists in Paris never get beyond that stage. They bike by necessity, not choice; they have left no cars behind them to boost their egos at crossroads confronta-

tions. They cycle religiously to their jobs as bank guards or post office clerks where they can take out their frustrations on the public. They use circle clips to keep their trousers clean and humble, they stop obediently at all traffic lights, they will press no more hardily on their pedals in order to respond to the challenge when you pass them. They are the *Lumpenproletariat* of traffic, prisoners on the bicycle chain gang.

My old black bicycle immediately placed me in their category. Those were the days before the minibike had been adopted at Saint-Tropez, thereby making it acceptable to miniminds in Paris. People unworthy of notice are never noticed by Parisians, a bicycle rider immediately becomes an invisible prole to most of them. Time and again, I would encounter a colleague and a secretary whiling away a lunch hour on Rue de la Gaîté in Montparnasse, but they looked right through me from behind the windows of his Merc. I let them go their gay way on Rue de la Gaîté (which has nothing to justify its name except for a self-service restaurant with the startling name of Self-Gaîté). I once turned up for work on a holiday and asked a guard for the key to an office, my own. The guard: "What for?" "Why, it's my office." The guard, hesitating, then: "Excuse me, *monsieur*, I always see you coming in on a bicycle. I thought you were manual." I assured him I was automatic and he gave me the key.

On Saturday afternoons, I would roam the city with my son. He was still under fourteen, too young to ride a Velosolex, that combination of bicycle and motor-cycle with all the disadvantages of both (the Velosolexist gets as little exercise as the motorist and as little protection as the cyclist). As soon as he became fourteen, I bought him a Solex and I didn't see him for five years. But in those days, we pedaled together through Paris. The city shrank before my eyes; gradually I realized how small its heart really is (the case of any large city where so much of the body is fat). From the Eiffel Tower to Notre Dame on a Saturday afternoon with my son used to be a whole Saturday afternoon by car. It turned out to be only twenty minutes by bike. We crossed the Seine over to the Proustian gardens of the Champs-Élysées, then got through the traffic on **Rue du Faubourg Saint-Honoré** by osmosis until the street lost its airs and its Faubourg to become Rue Saint-Honoré, bound for Les Halles napping in the afternoon. The markets were open then, now they have been put to sleep forever. From Les Halles, I could tow my son through forgotten alleys until we reached the Pont Neuf and the haven of Île de la Cité. We usually managed to take in the pet shops on the Right Bank—everything from monkeys to dyed chicks at Easter time—then the flower market on the island, before we got to Notre Dame.

By bicycle, that trip can be repeated time and again, it is never the same. I once made it with my niece and, lo and behold, there was a monkey up a tree on the edge of the flower market. Two firemen were up the tree with him, clambering about in their leather boots, shaking branches with a long stick while he clung for dear life until he let go to the gasps of the crowd, only to fall to safety onto a market shed. He could have skipped from shed to shed until the end of his days, but he was too much of a ham. He liked to hear the crowd gasp; he worked his way back to the tree that had become his territory while the firemen went after him again, encouraged by a *brigadier* who had gone up with them, all the better to survey the operation. My niece was only in Paris for a few weeks; I had trouble convincing her that I had not staged the whole thing as a happening for her benefit. She has grown up in one of the remote reaches of Queens, Long Island, known as Fresh Meadows, where there are no longer any meadows at all, fresh or stale. It is the kind of a place where the only thing that can happen is a happening.

I suppose that was what attracted me to the bicycle right from the start. It is not so much a way of getting somewhere as it is a setting for randomness; it makes every journey an unorganized tour. I remember one of the first days that I used it to go home to lunch. I was cutting down a wide avenue, with a mall in its middle, on market day. The market stalls were on the mall, the market men's trucks were parked diagonally to the curb, cars were backed up impatiently as a truck maneuvered out. I slithered by and got up to the truck. It was in the clear but the driver was talking to another marketeer, one of those **Paris** street conversations that drive waiting motorists to frenzy and their horns to crescendo. As I went by, the driver reached out to shake hands with his friend. I grabbed the dangling hand, shook it and went on. *"Salut, mon petit,"* he said.

He, too, must have thought I was manual. In any case, he did not think I belonged to that race of Parisians so hellbent on doing nothing that they will drive roughshod over anyone who gets in their way while he is engaged in doing something. It is so instructive to pull ahead of a lane of honking cars, mainly occupied by women late for their hairdressers or men late for their women, to weave through and find an Auvergnat unloading coal by the sack or a dairy truck discharging yogurt.

Only once did I escape the ninety-decibel blasts of the leisured. I had fallen in with Louis Carao, a bicycle cop in the 6th arrondissement who can handle any situation from a family quarrel to a traffic incident with irreproachable aplomb. He had beaten me in a sprint up the bus lane on Rue de Rennes despite his uniform and his police-issue bicycle and it was good to know that the peace of our neighborhood was in such capable hands and feet. We were riding side by side on Rue Vavin; a file of cars crawled behind us meek as cows, not a peep, not a beep, not a moo, the sight of Louis under his *képi* left them speechless. We rode and we talked; pedaling stimulates Louis's talking as it does my writing. He is a Breton, I am somewhat in his country when I ride through the farms around Lanloup and greet all the other Bretons who have not yet gone to Paris. They are Celts like the Irish and the Welsh; they belong to that doomed race of poets who have refused to take on the ways of the Franks or the Angles and the Saxons. In Brittany, there are more cyclists than I have seen anywhere else in France. The Parisians might say it is because the Bretons are

backward, I see nothing backward about the fine strapping women walking their bikes out of Lanvollon on market day, bread on the handlebars, meat and groceries on the back rack; the bike is a truck, a riding horse converted into a pack mule that has to be led.

It must be cycling that encouraged me to think as I do, to explore any turning that comes up, to take the unmarked roads to their end. That is the liberation that the bicycle can offer. I am more often for folkways than I am for bikeways. The bikeway is a start. It protects motor-man when he goes out for the first time without his tin shell. He feels so vulnerable; he can sense steel crushing his limbs the way it used to crush his fenders. But he should not stay too long on bicycle paths; there is no point in moving from one herd to another. The bicycle, in most places, is the only vehicle that does not carry a license plate. The cyclist has no "75" on his back in Paris, he need never display his social security number in Washington, he is considered so harmless that he is not required to carry insurance. Yet beware, a cyclist can go far. A few years back, a criminal involved in one of the unsuccessful attempts to assassinate de Gaulle managed to escape from his top-security prison on an island off the Channel coast. He got to the mainland; there a dragnet was cast for him. All roads were blocked, all cars were checked, the *autoroutes* coming into Paris were tied up for miles while police peered into trunks and pried under back seats. They never found their man; only later was it learned that he had reached Belgium by bicycle.

For the bicycle possesses ethereality, it floats along on those gossamer wheels that give themselves away only when they twinkle in the sun. The rider can violate the Heisenberg principle that the presence of the observer must necessarily change the phenomenon observed. The bicycle insinuates itself unseen into the innermost tissue of a large city where there is so, so much life that cannot be sensed through a windshield.

There are times in cities when they seem to emanate a flux. I have sensed it in Tokyo along lanes where cars have never entered, where the only vehicles were the two-wheeled trailers that the icemen towed behind their bicycles, stopping in front of the customer's door to saw off a cake for him. I would walk through festivals outside Shinto temples where the whole neighborhood was dancing to the sound of a drum mounted on a big wooden platform overhead, the drummer dancing as he swatted it. The bicycle had already taught me in Paris and New York that nothing could hurt me in places like this. I would venture into them for hours on end, never seeing a white face, thinking I had become yellow myself.

In Paris I once had the same feeling on an autumn afternoon near the Dugommier Métro station where an old man was running a merry-go-round. I had spotted him a few days before as I cruised by on my way to ride along the banks of the Marne. He had come with a wooden truck and trailer painted ever so long ago a robin's-egg blue. The truck went back to the war, the Great War, as the English call it, the days of 1914. The next time I rode by, the trailer had disappeared, its strange semi-circular sides had become the base of the merry-go-round, the little ride was all set up. Children in the neighborhood were sitting on Mickey Mouse or turning the wheel of a speedboat or honking the horn of a runabout while the merry-go-round spun round under the eyes of the old man, his skin bronzed by a lifetime outdoors on Place Dugommier or Boulevard de Belleville. There was a little park across the street on Rue de Charenton, the sun came slanting through the trees in the park, the merry-go-round and the park were one, held together by the sunbeams.

I talked to the old man and so did my friend the photographer. She was from the country around Tours in the valley of the Loire. He knew her country, he had played Touraine with his great airplane ride in 1912. He gave us his address and, on another day, we rode out there. He lived in Montrouge, a suburb on the southern border of Paris, one of the old suburbs where the country laps on the edge of the city, small houses and yards with chickens pecking in the dust and rabbits quietly fattening in their cages seven minutes by bicycle from Montparnasse. We recognized his place at once. The wood fence outside was the faded robin's-egg blue of the old Berliet truck, inside he lived in one of those circus trailers, a house on wheels. He was surrounded by all the trailers he had used in his life, they rusted and peeled as they grew old with him. He was well into his seventies, his hands trembled, but they could crank up the old chain-drive Berliet and put the Mickey Mouse figures into place on the merry-go-round. He was a stout house built long ago and still standing. When I returned to the trailer later to give him prints of the pictures we had taken, his daughter was there. She came once a week to clean the place. She told me her father had been a very strong man, she had seen him pick up an automobile and move it by himself.

His merry-go-round comes and goes on Place Dugommier when I ride by, it is part of the circuit that both of us ride through the forgotten quarters of Paris. I had lived twenty years in the city without ever seeing Place Dugommier and the merry-go-round. Inside a car in a city, your eyes are on the level of the garbage cans, they can see nothing else. Place Dugommier lies on Rue de Charenton, precisely the sort of street that the shrewd driver avoids. Rue de Charenton is clogged from early morning, when the garbage trucks come by with their tail of crawling cars, through the rest of the day as the furniture trucks load. It is one of the main streets of Faubourg Saint-Antoine, a part of Paris reputed for manufacturing dining-room sets and revolutions. Just off Rue de Charenton lies what must be the best market in Paris now that Les Halles are gone. Every day except Monday on Rue d'Aligre and Place d'Aligre, the pushcarts and the stands come out, their proprietors evenly divided between Algerian Arabs and former European settlers from Algeria, living together here with their shared memories. On Place d'Aligre, there is a *café-tabac* which, since it sells alcohol and cigarettes, is naturally the headquarters of the local sports club. I often come there for coffee in the morning, early in the morning when the cafés in Montparnasse are still asleep behind their barricades of chairs upended on tables. On Place d'Aligre, the market men and women arrive early; some breakfast on steaks, others on white wine. The *café-tabac* is open on Mondays as well, but then I have it almost to myself, sharing it with hand-truck drivers keeping their tanks topped up with wine. I never see Parlysian Parisians on Place d'Aligre and seldom on Rue de Charenton. They are too busy driving to their offices where they can work eleven months a year and dream of a month of picturesque living in a Club Méditerranée village only a few jet hours away on the shores of Morocco where there is an Arab quarter outside the well-guarded gate. They can see the Arabs, but the Arabs can't see them. The Club knows who its customers are. Every year when the weather gets hot and the traffic starts to stench in Paris, the big green city buses blossom out with signs on their rear ends: "Ah, if only you were with the Club Méditerranée . . ." Perhaps the Club pays the bus driver to squirt a little more diesel smoke when he carries the ad? It can be seen best from a following car. Pedestrians never look at it; on a bike, you never stay behind the bus long enough to get the message.

The bike in the city is ubiquitous. At one moment it can be on Place d'Aligre, at the next it can be on the Longchamp circuit in the Bois de Boulogne where the racers meet. That is also the meeting place of the same sort of semicyclist that one finds in Central Park in New York. He must take his racing bike to a bike path by car, he is afraid that he might be taken for carless if he did not. Yet Longchamp has its charms. You start riding until you catch someone or someone catches you. That does not take too long; the circuit is about two miles long around the outer fence of the Longchamp racetrack. You take turns slipstreaming, each of you push-ing along at top speed, until you catch up with someone. Then the two cyclists be-come a trio, the trio becomes a quartet and *und so weiter* until all the riders on the Longchamp circuit have been gathered up into a big flashing flock, their stock-inged legs, blue, red, green, pumping up and down, up and down, like pistons; their feet attached to the pedals so that their ankles work like bearings, the big wheels with the chrome spokes winking at the sun, sending motes over blue, green, red stockings. It is almost impossible to shake off a cyclist once he's in your wake; you fight the wind, he just goes along for the ride.

There is one little fellow at Longchamp who can leave me behind. He uses a lini-ment to warm up his thigh muscles and it lays a barrage of reek right behind his rear wheel. No one can get near him; he rushes around Longchamp at the head of the flock, invincible in his liniment. We can only pick him up on the backstretch where the wind turns; now it buoys us along, we whir at twenty-five miles per hour as if we were sitting in our living rooms; the air is still, the Flying Skunk loses most of his advantage, we can put him behind.

But if there is no wind, then I usually let him have Longchamp all to himself. I spin out at the Porte de Boulogne, I fight the nonorganic exhaust stink on Saint-Cloud bridge leading to the Autoroute de l'Ouest and, from there, I head straight up into the Parc de Saint-Cloud, one of the handsome vestiges of the royal forests that used to stretch from Paris to Versailles and beyond. The Parc de Saint-Cloud is cer-tainly the quietest, wildest, and yet the most beautiful park on the western end of

Paris (a situation that is to be remedied by cutting a new freeway through an area where only the squirrels can protest).

It is a favorite haunt of Parisian drivers and their dogs. Many *automobilistes* tend to travel with gigantic mastiffs in the car, a fashion probably set by women cab drivers. These beasts glare at you from the back seat; one deterred me from passing his master in a tight spot because he had all his fangs bared, waiting to tear a piece out of an unwary cyclist just as the shark keeps an eye out for the passing scuba diver. When the car stops, the Parisian leaves his dog inside. He does not believe in such Anglo-Saxon nonsense as being kind to animals unless his girl friend happens to be wearing some. Thanks to man's best friend, the parked car can be noisier in Paris than the moving car when a pent-up dog begins to growl, then to howl. He wakes up the neighborhood, he's as bad as a stuck horn but with a difference: the stuck horn won't take your finger off if you try to fix it. The poor dog yowls inside the car until his master drives him off to a restaurant where he can then howl, growl, and yowl from under the table at all the other hungry dogs in the establishment. In a Parisian restaurant, dogs go hungry, there are no doggy bags, the lords and masters wolf all the food, there are no leftovers. Some Parisian dog lovers, appalled at the Biafra-like misery at their feet, have trained their animals to snap up Camembert rinds. Restaurants have a way of getting quieter about the time of the cheese course.

To keep his dog in trim, the Parisian takes him to the Parc de Saint-Cloud. He doesn't walk him, he drives him. I witnessed the process one Sunday morning in the *parc*. On a pleasant stretch where a one-lane road climbs through birch woods, I was tooted and passed by a little red Fiat station wagon. Behind the little red Fiat bounded a little white fox terrier. He passed me, too; I labored up the hill after shifting down about seven or eight speeds. I thought I could catch him once I began to run downhill. I wheezed over the summit, fiddled with the gearshift levers and soon I was helling downhill on my private asphalt ski run, bent way over the handlebars to cut the wind resistance. When I really want to go fast, I bow my head. I don't know if this streamlines me, but I don't get the wind in my eyes and so I think I'm fighting it less. A friend of mine who used to do some amateur racing can get his head down so far that his backside is higher than his neck, giving him that egg shape so sought after by schussers. I'm too tall and stiff, I can't get any closer than a scrambled egg. At any rate, I egged myself on down the hill, down I tore, not a sign of the Fiat through the bare birches on that winter Sunday. I leaned into a curve to take it without braking. That's the most fearsome part of running downhill. If you lean far enough, you can go around anything, but your whole body screams that it doesn't want to lean. You must sneak up on it, tip it by surprise, don't watch the outer edge of the asphalt or you'll break up.

The road came out of the birches into a clearing. The little red Fiat was parked on the shoulder, a little blue man in a blue track suit was getting out to jog, the little white fox terrier was standing next to a log, not even breathing hard. As I went by, he cocked a leg up to show what he thought of his competition.

I coasted to the bottom of the hill, I started to climb again. Once more a toot, a deeper note, a big gray Citroën with a hound of some sort loping behind it like a footman behind a royal coach. This time, the driver took the whole circuit and I caught him just at the bottom of the hill where he had opened the lid of the trunk to put the dog back in.

I stopped, smiled, and said: "Don't you think you need the exercise as much as your *chien* does?"

He stopped, smiled, and said: "But, *monsieur,* I am now going off to jog five kilometers at the Racing Club. And this is a *chienne.*" He didn't have to tell me, any fool could have seen that, just looking at the dog. I smiled and said: "I know, *monsieur,* but I am an American and I always mix my genders in French." That excused everything; he confided to me with pride in English that his bitch could keep up twenty-five kilometers an hour for nearly five kilometers. I congratulated him, I petted the dog, and I cycled off humbled. You must hand it to the Parisians, they've found a way for man to replace the mechanical rabbit. Such are the discoveries that are needed in our time if we are to give people something to do in between vacations.

In my cycling through Central Park in New York, I have never met anyone pacing a small dog with a large car. The trails of the park near 59th Street are not recommended for cycling in the early morning. They are filled by people walking dogs, big dogs; you have the impression that somebody opened the cages in the zoo. These dogs are as useful to the Manhattan city dweller as their ancestors were to the caveman. Big and fierce enough to stop a young urban riot on the strength of their appearance alone, they allow their owners to feel perfectly safe walking in Central Park. Such dogs, of course, *must* be walked in Central Park if they are to keep in the kind of shape required to awe the indigenous fauna. This keeps their masters in shape; here we find man and animal living harmoniously, like the pilot fish and the shark, the little bird that likes rhinoceroses, the dog and the flea.

I quickly became discouraged while riding through this menagerie in Central Park, the dogs sizing me up, the masters tugging back at the reins as if they were trying to stop runaway horses. Only once has anyone ever looked at me in Paris the way those dogs scrutinized me in New York. With my bicycle, I had wandered into the meat shed at Les Halles, just for the sake of wandering. I liked the sight of those clean white and red carcasses on their hooks in long straight ranks, looking like soldiers standing formation except that they are already dead. As I stopped at the head of a row to take it all in, a wholesaler looked at me. He was one of those men with small eyes and big bellies native to the meat shed at Les Halles. He looked me in the eye, he looked at my feet, and, suddenly, I had the feeling that he was calculating how much I would fetch, skinned and dressed. Not very much; he soon turned away.

In New York, too, I prowl the city in the early hours. Before the cars are out, there is not that much difference between Paris and New York. There is the same rich core only a few minutes in diameter by bicycle. From Herald Square to the Battery is only twenty minutes and at least five different cultures: Big Town, China-town, Little Italy, Spanishtown on 14th Street, Georgetown over in the West Vil-lage.

I would start a trip to the Battery at five in the morning. I would rise stealthily and, without awakening my mother in whose Park Avenue apartment I was staying, I would take my bicycle from her seventh-floor balcony and go out the door. I had been told by all concerned, superintendent, doormen, elevator men (it's one of *those* Manhattan buildings, all it lacks is a draw-bridge and a password) that I would be foolhardy to leave the bike in the cellar or the lobby. So I took it upstairs every night, the way people used to do in Paris during the Occupation. Around dinnertime, there would usually be people in the elevator and the bike made a fine conversation piece, especially if there were four or five other passengers and I had to stand it on its back wheel to make room for them. While the back wheel of the bike fraternized with their dogs, I would chat with the owners.

"That sure beats the traffic, doesn't it?"

"It sure does."

"Oh, I get off here, 'night."

" 'Night."

The quality of the night elevator man's conversation was much higher. He puzzled me, the way he used words accurately, al-most artificially. Early next morning, when I came down with the bike, I happened to mention to him that I had a better bike in France where I lived.

"Oh, you live in France? I'm French."

"You're French?"

"Yes, my name is John Martin . . . *Jean Martin.*"

We slipped into French. He explained to me he had no intention of going back to France. He was earning over a hundred dollars a week as a *liftier de nuit,* his wife was earning the same. They had been able to go on spending like Frenchmen while earning like Americans, *la vie* was *belle.* Jean-John Martin didn't mind running an elevator up and down as long as he didn't have to run around in circles. He was a contented man.

"You know what Merleau-Ponty told Sartre at the Café des Deux Magots, don't you?" Monsieur Martin asked me. I re-membered vaguely that Merleau-Ponty had played high priest to Sartre's pope when existentialism flowered in Saint-Germain-of-the-Meadows. Sartre was and still is the leader of the Left Bank Left, the militant minks, the starving intellectuals (no pota-toes, no bread, no starches, no sauces, no fats, just beautiful bones), the last-ditch fighters against Yankee imperialism who boldly snap their fingers at decadent pluto-cratic racist Uncle Sam by driving Lancias and BMWs instead of Chevrolets or Mus-tangs.

I didn't know what Merleau-Ponty told Sartre at the Café des Deux Magots . . . unless he was trying to get him to pick up the check. I shook my head as we reached the ground floor and started to wheel my bike out through the lobby.

"He said: 'Do you know what I'll do if the Communists ever take over in France?'

"Sartre said: 'No, what will you do?'

"And Merleau-Ponty said: 'I'll go to New York and become an elevator man.' "

Monsieur Martin looked around expansively at the building lobby, the engravings of old Murray Hill, the carpet, not a soul in sight, the world dark and empty outside the plate-glass doors.

"Eh bien, me voilà!"

I left him in his air-conditioned reverie and headed south along Fifth Avenue at half past five in the morning. A very safe time to be in the streets of New York, the traffic isn't out and the muggers are all in. Cycling is pleasant, you need only keep a weather eye out for the privately owned garbage trucks that rumble and race through the streets with their cargoes of expensive aromas from the restaurants of lower Manhattan. They are big bruising hulking vehicles with the bulk of a tank and the acceleration of a Honda. I gave them plenty of room as they made their U-turns to go the wrong way down one-way streets.

South I rode along Fifth Avenue, then onto Broadway where the twain met. The streets got into the low numbers. I didn't have to worry about directions, I let Broadway find the way. I just kept my head down, not for speed but for safety. My eyes were glued to the surface; there are holes in the streets of New York, holes the like of which I have never seen elsewhere. They could swallow up a small Citroën, they would not even make a tidbit of a large bicycle. In the United States, country roads are smooth and manicured, the cities are full of holes. In France, it is Paris that enjoys hand-paved streets while the peasants bounce along the ruts and crevasses that break out on all roads except those where tolls are charged. In New York, too, there are gratings over sewers where the gap between the

bars is narrow enough to let a bus go over them safely, but easily wide enough to gulp the front wheel of a bike. All the hazards of New York are on such a scale.

At Union Square, there was an island of slight activity, bums stirring on the benches, a jogger or two stamping around the park. Then back to the dark again, the numbers on the streets changing to names, down through the incredible no man's land between Lower Fifth Avenue and Lower Manhattan—seedy sleazy lofts, blocks and blocks, the world's crummiest structures next to the world's most expensive real estate, discount houses and Army and Navy stores, the Peaceful Army and Navy Store.

From the Empire State Building to the Battery is a quick run at half past five in the morning or at any time of the day. Infiltrating traffic is easy in New York; in Paris you must keep an alert eye for the door that suddenly opens in your face. Sometimes it is attached to the high cab of a truck at the level of your neck and calculated to leave you rolling down to the next traffic light, a headless torso, blood spouting from the stump in a neat many-streamed fountain.

Americans never open their car doors in New York. They go through the city locked into their Apollo spaceships, air conditioners turned on to preserve the temperature, humidity, barometric pressure, and political opinions of Westchester, air conditioners leaving a searing wake of heat behind their cars like the exhaust from a Saturn booster; dark glass on their windshields to protect them from looking the facts of urban life straight in the eye.

At the Battery that morning, I rode up to

the car lane of the Staten Island Ferry. The black man in the ticket window gave me change for a dollar, all in nickles. When I asked him when the next boat would leave, he told me to look at the schedule posted outside.

I knew it would happen, New York had been invaded by the Parisians.

I rode to the head of the car lanes as I always do, there's never a wait for the cyclist at the Staten Island Ferry. That morning, only two trucks were on line, their drivers asleep over their wheels. A ferry was in and unloading. A minute later, the gates were open and I slipped aboard, riding through the tunnel of the empty car hold until I reached the bow. There, I locked the bike to a stanchion. At one time, I thought the Staten Island Ferry was the only place in New York where you could leave a bike unlocked with a fair chance of finding it when you came back, but a deck hand disagreed. "Better chain that thing up, one of those juiceheads might come along and throw it overboard."

I went topside and, at the food stand, I took a large orange juice in a paper cup and went out on deck. There, standing at the rail, I toasted the rising sun, the towers of Manhattan, the Verrazano Bridge, the Con Ed smokestack that was just sneaking out its first oily layers of blackish smoke to flatten against the hot sky when no one was awake to look. I toasted Governor's Island, Ellis Island, a tugboat named Moran, a railroad-car ferry, the Statue of Liberty. I got to feeling possessive about that ferry. I used to take it almost every morning when I was in New York for a short visit. A little later on another morning, I was drinking my orange juice next to a little boy. I breathed the air of New York Bay, not too deeply because the wind was coming from New Jersey. I turned to him and I said:

"You know, this is my yacht."

The wheels began to click in his head. He looked out at the water, he looked back at Manhattan on fire in the sun, his eyes caught the Statue of Liberty, then he turned to me and he said:

"It's mine, too."

He was a lot smarter than another kid about the same age who was making the trip with his daddy. This little boy noticed a long spar that might have been a flagpole except that it happened to be jutting out at a forty-five-degree angle from the base of the pilothouse.

His father, an Irishman, squinted up and produced an immediate answer:

"Oh, that's their harpoon. They carry it just in case they see a whale in the bay."

I wasn't as dumb as that kid. When the ferry was pulling in, I asked the first mate what was that big stick up there. He said it was a steering staff: since a ferry has no bow, somebody had to put a fixed point in front of the pilot so he could line his ship up on where he was going.

Ferryboats are conducive to conversation if the ride lasts long enough, as it does on New York Bay. On still another occasion, I was standing up forward with my bike. A young man had just gotten out of his car, a red Opel. He was unhappy because he had missed the previous boat; they hadn't held it for him and now he was going to be late for his job driving a big semitrailer for the U.S. Post Office up on 33rd Street.

62

He didn't mind the job, but the pay wasn't too good, he couldn't afford more than an Opel. He had already passed the examination for the Department of Sanitation and he was waiting for the first opening so that he could make the change. It wasn't as bad as it looked, he explained. On a garbage truck, there are three men, all drivers. Each one takes his turn driving every third day. The other two days, he rides along on the back.

"It's a Civil Service job, just like the Post Office, but you can go out on strike. And it pays way over ten thousand a year."

A pause.

"The only trouble is, two days out of three, you've got to handle that garbage."

Chapter 6

THE EYE OF THE CYCLE

The world lies right beyond the handlebars of any bicycle that I happen to be on anywhere from New York Bay to the Vallée de Chevreuse. Anywhere is high adventure, the walls come down, the cyclist is a loner, it is the only way for him to meet other loners. And it works. One seldom exchanges anything but curses or names of insurance companies with another driver, the car inhibits human contacts. The bicycle generates them; bikes talk to each other like dogs, they wag their wheels and tinkle their bells, the riders let their mounts mingle. On the road, you can join any club of cyclists in France, there is no membership fee. Stay with them on the hills and take your turn up front upwind, that's all the initiation ceremony there is.

It is wise to avoid racers. The best company is a mixed bag of all ages, youngsters for sprints, the fifties and even the sixties for endurance. I know one such group that meets at nine o'clock every Sunday morning at the Montrouge town hall just beyond Porte de Châtillon on the south side of

Paris. Like so many hundreds of others on Sunday morning, they head out into the Chevreuse Valley, the closest countryside to the city. It has everything on a cycle scale: hills, plateaus, woods, plains, rivers, villages, steeples. If you want to see the Chevreuse Valley from a bicycle seat, just turn up at the Montrouge town hall and follow the crowd past Châtenay-Malabry where a statue of Voltaire smiles down on you, across Route 186 throwing its girdle of steel and smog around the outer suburbs of Paris, through the greenhouses and the orchards of Verrières le Buisson and then into the Chevreuse Valley.

Montrouge rolls winter and summer, rain or shine. On the Sunday that I joined them, the weather was cold and dry in Paris but, as soon as we got beyond Verrières, the roads ran wet with drainage from farms. The back wheel of my racing bike, stripped of its mudguard to gain an extra few ounces, was picking water from the road and, with every turn, sending it up my back, from fundament to the nape of my neck, a wet muddy swath along my spine. I looked as if I had been sitting on one of those superbidets used in Spain and Portugal according to the law that the more Catholic the country, the stronger the sitz-plumbing.

At this point, we had reached the state of happy equilibrium that the cyclist achieves in winter when he is soaking wet with sweat, rain, and mud but he has heated the whole mixture to 98.4° F. or so and it lubricates more than anything else. The merry men from Montrouge rolled merrily . . . until a shot rang out. It was one of our wheelmates blowing a tubular, a *boyau,* the French call it, the word means gut. You put about seventy pounds of pressure in it; when you blow a gut, you can hear it half a mile off.

We stopped. He unrolled his spare gut kept in a package under his seat. The wind that had been on our heels caught us, it blew through the sweat and the wet, it turned them to chill and slime. Our noses trickled and icicled, our hands froze red and blue as we stretched that tubular, almost tearing a gut, until we got it over the rim. Once it was in place, we helped him blow up his gut. Off we rolled, fifty yards, a hundred yards, we stopped again, the tire was coming off the rim. Tubulars should be cemented, we had no cement. We went through the stretch-and-freeze all over again, the tubular was back on the wheel, but it had to be treated warily. So we started slowly downhill, exerting no effort, building up no heat in our furnaces, while the wind tore at us with renewed glee and our noses ran as wet as the tar beneath our wheels.

It was there that, once again, I felt the barrier of a pane of glass. Automobiles went by, loaded with families sitting motionless in their warmth, huddled inside their wombs. We could have been on the moon and they on the earth, though only two or three feet separated us on the cold road. Our feet moved automatically, instinctively; we could not feel them any longer, they had been stuck out in a freezing mist for a couple of hours with no more protection than the skin-deep leather of cyclists' shoes the weight of ballet slippers and perhaps some newspaper. Round and round our feet churned; we could not have told you if our legs were driving the bicycles or the bicycles were driving the legs. Some of the auto nobility in the passing cars smiled at us, others ignored us the way I had always been taught to ignore cripples, beggars, unshaven men asking directions, staring at them as if they did not exist. On one and the same road, they were going out for Sunday dinner and we were trying to reach the North Pole over the ice floes and through the watery chasms. They would not have believed us if we had told them. They knew that the North Pole had already been discovered; they could not have known that it was just outside their windows in the Chevreuse Valley.

Exploration comes easy on a bicycle, the unknown is everywhere. Once, with the photographer, I was cycling early in the morning over the black flat landscape of the Gatinais country just north of Orléans. We flicked out our lights, we could see better without them and the generators took too much of our strength. A bicycle headlight will only cover ten feet of road; even at fifteen miles an hour, that's not enough. So we used our lights as markers, starting the generators whenever we saw or heard a car, then back to darkness again. Without lights on a strange road, the sensation was almost of flying. We could see ahead, we could not see at our feet. We had to hope no boulders had been strewn in our path, that no New York–sized potholes pocked the way.

It was worth the risk. Villages in Gatinais are few and far between by French standards, one only every five miles or so. We steered from one farmhouse to the next, their lights standing out like those of an island in the sea. That day, I guess, we rounded Cape Horn by bicycle. We got as far as Bishop's Ford Pond, then we came back against the wind, through the Roaring Forties. The sun was up, we could see the houses now; the white sheets drying on the lines bellied like the sails of a square-rigger running downwind; we dipped our heads in salute as we beat our way back to town where housewives were sweeping the sidewalk in front of their doors, dipping their brooms into the water that had been sent

coursing through the gutters from a municipal tap. All the women in town were out together at dawn, scrubbing their sidewalks. We tried to photograph them; it was too late by the time we had enough light, the tap had been turned off and the ball was over. We went to a café to breakfast on bread and black tea while the owner's dog leaped all over us. French country dogs are as nice as French country people, they have nothing in common with the yapping poodle or the trembling Mexican hairless native to Paris. The dogs are friendly in the little hotels that the bicycle sniffs out: *Au Petit Chalet, Au Moulin Vert,* the *Relais du Saôsnois,* the *Hostellerie de la Vallée du Lunain;* I keep their cards, occasionally their modest bills, just to remind myself that money isn't everything, that in fact it is nothing, it is a hurdle that makes the pursuit of happiness an obstacle course.

O blessed bicycles, they can scent out the places where I have no business—the pretentious dump on 42nd Street where

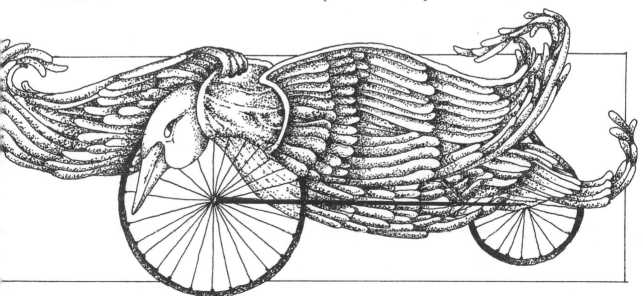

there is no room to park a bike and the night clerk offers service with a snarl. I spent a night there, the next morning I straddled a bicycle and let it have its head. It took me round the edges of Manhattan, the frayed hem of what used to be the waterfront. Down to South Street, around Battery Park, once Castle Garden and the Aquarium, now a beach for bums and others who want to be left alone. No one stares at them there except the binocular telescopes mounted on the rim of the park; their eyepieces eyes, their fittings facial expressions, you can cock them in their swivels to create attitudes for a photographer in the early morning. I rolled past the fireboat pier, pure 1900 Luna Park, past the big bollards where the tugs tie up and wait to taxi harbor pilots out to their ships. The express liners are gone, the great changing skyline of New York's waterfront —the four stacks of the *Mauretania* and the *Aquitania,* the grace of the *Europa* and the *Bremen.* We once sailed from the Battery on a tug to greet my dad on the *Bremen* when she lay off in quarantine. I remember the icebox cake on that tug; every time I roll by the Battery I always look into the galleys of the tugs tied up there to see what they are serving.

In 1967, I sailed past the Battery myself on the *France* outward bound; the *Queen Elizabeth* was following us a mile astern. Down the Hudson we paraded, no festive occasion, nothing more than an Atlantic crossing; you could have got the passenger lists of both ships into a clutch of 747s. Off Sandy Hook, we slowed to drop the pilot. His cutter was waiting out there to pick up the pilots as they finished their runs, it was

a trysting place for ships. The *France* lost way, she lay still, the pilot stepped into his bobbing boat; now the *Queen Elizabeth* was drawing near, coming up out of the haze. Our pilot was clear, the black smoke poured from the funnels of the *France,* scouring out the fuel oil that had clogged the pipes in port; she showed her *derrière* to Queen Elizabeth, Trafalgar was avenged. Now the *Queen Elizabeth* stopped to drop her pilot at the same spot chalked on the sea by the choreographer; we lost her from sight, we will never see her again, we will only see the phantoms of the city of stacks as we cycle up West Street past the shattered piers, up North River.

A good way up, well out of the desolation zone where the World Trade Center is encroaching on the river, I came across a place that proclaimed itself a motel. It didn't look like a motel, it looked like a scale model of the Flatiron Building, a sailors' rooming house, perhaps, that had somehow survived the departure of the sailors. On one side of its prow lay the piers, on the other a street of wholesale meat markets. I walked in; behind a pane of bulletproof glass, a spry little lady was sitting. I asked her if she had any rooms, and, in a Scottish accent that she had not lost in fifty years, she replied that she had. I could take my bicycle up there, too, for the same price. She apologized—I had to pay in advance. Up at 42nd Street, I had to pay in advance, too, but nobody apologized. That hotel was close to the United Nations, my motel *was* the United Nations: the manager was Iranian, the day clerk Scottish, the night clerk Filipino; there was good Cuban company among the butchers who took their dawn coffee at a diner a block away, a true diner not ashamed of its trolley-car lineage. The lady serving coffee was heavy and warm; she told of how she used to work uptown near the ships. All the sailors knew the place, they would invite her aboard the *Normandie* or the *Andrea Doria* for their Christmas parties in port. It was all gone, she said, the waterfront was a ghost town. I had bought a ticket for New York, I had ended up in Leadsville, Colorado. The lady may have known the seamen who sailed my dad across, she may have known Yves, the old oiler on the *Île de France* who stays gently oiled on weekends at the Duvals' café in Brittany. Once he has got steam up, he tells all Lanloup what life is like in New York. The chickens drop into your hands already roasted from a slot in the wall; nobody buys a newspaper, they stand in the streets and read the news for nothing as it flashes in lights around a building. "Right, *monsieur?*" he asked me, his fellow American. Right, I say, as I head away from the café on my bicycle.

I often start from cafés. The photographer and I know so many cafés in Paris that each must think it is our favorite. The owner of the Escurial on Boulevard Saint-Germain likes to talk to me about cycling as I wait for the photographer. I always park my bike next to his oyster stand, still deserted at six in the morning, so that I can keep an eye on both the bike and the street as I wait.

One morning as I talked to the owner, the photographer arrived, black slacks, black sweater, black parka (on really important occasions, she ties her hair with a red ribbon from a candy box), a white bike. I said good-bye to the owner and started to sprint for the saddle. "Ah, *monsieur,*" he said, "cycling is truly your passion."

The photographer and I headed east along Boulevard Saint-Germain. She rode her bicycle as if she were gliding. Once she had got up speed, she spread her arms wide and moved them up and down as easily as a gull moves its wings. She was a bird, soaring along the boulevard, the light of her headlight dancing in the silvery spokes of her front wheel. The spokes chopped up the light to send it whirling in a gold-silvery swoop. A remote cousin of mine once told me he saw something like that when he looked at the spray from the hose on the lawn of his parents' suburban home in New Jersey after he had taken acid. I like bike trips myself.

The photographer was a big black bird on her bicycle. Or she was a mahout. She told me that when she held the handlebars, the round white rubber grips with the little holes at their ends, they felt like an elephant's trunk. She was a mahout, leading two elephants down Boulevard Saint-Germain. I rode at her side, trying to protect her from the odd car speeding down the boulevard at this odd hour.

We kept riding east, into the rising sun that was lined up perfectly with the street as if Boulevard Saint-Germain had been constructed by worshippers of Ra. In truth, it had been built by Baron Haussmann, the great city planner of the 1860s who put the urban freeways of his day into the city of Paris. Boulevard Saint-Germain is one of the clearways that the security-minded Haussmann tore through old Paris, too

68

wide to be barricaded and ruler-straight to give artillery an easy shot at the mob.

Technology caught up with Haussmann when overturned cars and buses blocked his sociological fire lanes in May 1968 as thoroughly as they do right side up in every other month and year. He had not reckoned with a society that would provide its protesters not only with the raw material to erect instant barricades but the gasoline to convert them at will into fire bombs. The cops finally got their counterdeterrent, an armored bulldozer that sliced through the piled-up cars, doing only slightly more damage than if the students had been allowed to use up their energy in futile shadowboxing.

No barricade withstood such assaults in May and June 1968, no barricade save one that I saw outside the medical school on Rue des Saints-Pères that intersects Boulevard Saint-Germain. The medical students there had parked a loaded garbage truck across the street, sealing it off. The police didn't dare overturn the stewing marinating mess (something really must be rotten before a Parisian will throw it out) and, *a fortiori,* the students didn't go near it, either. It was the absolute defense against riot control but, as happens usually and fortunately in such cases, its deterrent power was so awesome that it never had to be used. Since the police didn't go near it, there was no riot. When no one was looking the students drove it away before the sun and the garbage got too high.

The photographer and I rode past Rue des Saints-Pères and followed Boulevard Saint-Germain as it imperceptibly changes the lift of its eyebrows and the tilt of its nostrils from Saint-Germain-des-Prés to

the Latin Quarter. All these changes are measured in yards. We rode past a little hotel where the manager is Vietnamese; the price is outrageous but there is a sixth-floor room with a balcony where you can see the sun rise along the axis of Boulevard Saint-Germain.

The boulevard runs near the Seine. But it is straight and the Seine winds, so the two must meet somewhere. They do, at Pont Sully right below Pont d'Austerlitz (the reason why so few new bridges are built in Paris is that there haven't been too many victories since Austerlitz). Pont Sully hops across the Seine, using the end of Île Saint-Louis, as a stepping stone. I like the way Paris built its old bridges. They move gingerly over the river in their stone boots, suspicious of water (both salt and fresh, as all Frenchmen are except the seafaring Bretons). When the Seine grows high, the boots become boats, breasting the current with a foaming bow wave.

The photographer and I turned left where Boulevard Saint-Germain drowns itself in the Seine. We started to cross Pont Sully, named after Maximilien de Béthune, Duke of Sully (1559–1641), minister of King Henri IV (1553–1610). In death as well as life, Sully serves his sovereign. Pont Sully leads into Boulevard Henri IV, which ends at the Bastille just as the Ancien Régime did. The word *régime* also means "a diet" in French, which may help you to understand a slogan I once saw painted on a wall near the Sorbonne: REGIME GAULLISTE = REGIME AMAIGRISSANT.

Amaigrissant means thinning, the verb is the root of our word "meager." It is amazing how many English words now entering French as despised "Franglais" originally came from French, words like *le management* that is only the good French word *ménager* in disguise. But no Franglais is needed on the walls of Paris, French is alive there. Right near the Sorbonne wall where I saw the comment about the Gaullist regime I spotted another that said, "POMPIDOU IS A DIRTY CAPITALIST." An editor had come along to make a change: he crossed out "dirty" and wrote in "clean." The walls have voices, I can hear them in Paris when I try to get to work on my bicycle.

That is not always easy. My bike hates to go to work. It is an aquaphile, it prefers to follow the water—rivers and canals inland, hard sand on tidal beaches by the sea. The grades are easier there, hill-climbing is no problem along a waterfront or a canal. Life began along the rivers, it prospered with the canals. Much of that life is still preserved there even around cities the size of Paris or New York or Washington. Canals are smack in the middle of the eighteenth century, they belong to Louis XV or George Washington. They carry their life with them; their people are isolated high up on the levees, lock-keepers in lonely houses, the towpath running under the trees, the bike swishing through gravel where horses once plodded.

That is why my bicycle always heads over Pont Sully towards the Bastille, then east on Rue de Charenton toward the Marne. The Seine is a big river for Paris; the city stretches for miles along its banks, you need a car to get away. Not the Marne; it is winding and secretive; the barges avoid part of it by taking a canal that runs through a tunnel just outside Paris. That leaves the river pretty much to its own re-

sources. Distances along the Marne are within a cyclist's reach. About fifteen minutes from the Latin Quarter and he is in the Bois de Vincennes, the eastern pendant of the Bois de Boulogne, but stark and deserted by those who want to be seen because they would not be seen dead in the Bois de Vincennes. Consequently, the Bois de Vincennes is alive with kite-flyers, cyclists, skippers of model yachts, wild duck colonies, rugby teams, cross-country runners, trotting horses, bettors, rookie cops in training, a rundown cartridge factory used as a theater for touring troupes, a military firing range, a vast hidden statue of Beethoven, quite a *bois*. On its far side, Nogent-sur-Marne starts, a suburb that thinks it's a beach resort, it even looks like a beach resort. It has a yacht harbor all its own with a lighthouse and a stretch of gravel beach much quieter than the Croisette at Cannes. The Marne is not recommended for swimming around Nogent, but I wouldn't recommend the Mediterranean around Cannes, either. The same process that destroyed river beaches a skip away from the city of Paris and drove swimmers to the sea has now worked its way to the sea itself.

Just before Nogent, the barges come back to the Marne after their tunnel. I know a road along the Marne, in some places it is tarred, in others it is a muddy path, that follows the barges as they buck the river east of Paris. On winter mornings, I can watch them from shore on my bike just above the mist laid over the water like icing on a cake. Like almonds in the icing, the pilothouses of the barges stick up from the mist, disembodied superstructures without hulls.

I can follow the barges about six miles up the river. Coming into Bry-sur-Marne, there is an island in the middle of the river, Île des Loups, Wolves' Island. The houses along its banks are magnificent, they stand in splendid isolation, accessible only by boat. There are no roads on the island, a railroad viaduct puts one leg of an arch on the west end, but islanders cannot cross on the tracks. The shore of the island is screened by trees. When they are in leaf, the houses are gone. There is only a sliver of forest in mid-Marne, that was why wolves lived on Wolves' Island.

One day in November—it was on one of those long five-day weekends that the French school system sets aside to keep children in their parents' hair—a barge went by, a brown-hulled barge running close to the shore of the island, almost under the trees. Up at the bow, a little girl was skipping rope. She was dressed in a pleated navy-blue skirt and a matching sweater; those were her holiday clothes. She had come home to the barge from her boarding school for the vacation, and her mother had told her to go out and play in the yard where her father could keep an eye on her from the pilot house as he steered the family house. The green mansions of Wolves' Island slid by the brown-hulled barge and the little girl in navy blue as she skipped rope. Round and round the rope flew under her feet and over her head, thwacking the deck, keeping time perhaps to the beat of the propeller that was thrashing away in the stern, thwacking the Marne as a housewife thwacks her laundry. I followed her a while from the bank, making no noise, stealthy as a wolf, watching the little girl on her moving playground, the rope flying, her feet never missing a skip. Then the river road turned into a mess of mudded ruts and I had to look down at my wheels as the barge sailed away from me on the smooth Marne, the little girl and her jump rope still in the bow.

At Bry-sur-Marne, there is an iron footbridge that was built in 1894, so the plaque at its base reads, by the local mayor whose name has long since vanished from nearly everywhere else on the face of the earth. You climb a flight of stone steps to the top of the bridge. It is no great feat to take a racing bike up the steps with you. For those riding heavier mounts, there is a strip of cement next to the steps, just wide enough to fit the wheels of a Velosolex or a light Honda. A boathouse is boarded up, the name of its proprietor has turned a pastel whitish-pink; he probably went out of the boating business as the Marne lost its fresh bloom of youth. When the fish start floating belly up in a river, nobody wants to swim in it face down. So the boathouse closed and so did the swimming dock at the foot of the footbridge. Too bad, there is a fine little beach down there, soft sand and an easy slope into the water.

A plank walk crosses the top of the bridge, then there are the same steps leading down the other side. There is a restaurant on the left bank run by a big cheerful man in overalls who sympathizes with my lot as a cyclist because he used to be a motorcycle cop. His restaurant reminds me of one of those old ocean liners with three or four classes. You can stand in the bar and match Pernods with the boss, you can dine in one of the more elegant rooms where the locals come with their dressed-up wives and their fed-up children, or you can eat with the regulars at one of the tables in the bar, table d'hôte, no menu.

Often, on Sundays, I ride out through the Bois de Vincennes and I make the restaurant at Bry in an easy hour or so, thereby solving such multifarious problems as where to eat Sunday dinner, where to go for a Sunday ride, and how to get back home without Sunday traffic. The regulars at their single tables sit in a row facing the bar, their backs to the Marne outside the big glass doors.

When the weather is good, you can eat out in the garden on steel tables and chairs right next to your bicycle. I took the photographer there once. We crossed the footbridge, parked our bikes in the garden next to the river and sat down while the waitress took our orders. As she was serving the *pâté,* a barge hove in sight.

The photographer raced up the steps of the footbridge to look at the barge. Barges must be seen from above as well as from the side. Nearly every one that goes by has a collection of hens, roosters, and rabbits in its cargo of sand. The hens peck, the roosters crow, the rabbits hop, and the whole barnyard sails past the towers of Notre Dame, the turrets of the Conciergerie, the cold elegance of the Quai d'Orsay, the pricey heights of Passy looking down on the rest of the city from their lofty standard of living, the new riverfront quarter of Beaugrenelle with its fifteen-story "skyscraper" apartment houses, identical in shape, identical in size. The Parlysians keep putting up buildings that look like troops standing at attention for years, never batting a Venetian blind as the sooty rain acidly etches into their concrete, streaking the walls, cracking the cornices,

the same buildings all over the city and the suburbs, at Beaugrenelle on the Seine, at Bois d'Arcy and Ris-Orangis where the Bronx has been transplanted to farmers' fields with cows all around, at Bagnolet for workers, at Garches for young executives, on the hills of Belleville and Ménilmontant in what was once the cocky tarty Paris that Maurice Chevalier sang.

These are the ideas that can come to mind as I sit in a river garden and watch a barge pass. I nibbled at the *pâté,* waiting for the photographer to come down from the bridge. She didn't come down; I finished the *pâté,* mine and some of hers, I took a sip of wine from the earthenware pitcher. Still she didn't come down. What was left of her *pâté* was getting warm, soon the waitress would bring out the roast pork and it would be getting cold.

I got up from the table, crossed the road, and walked up the steps of the bridge. She was not at the railing, she was on all fours in the middle of the plank walk, her rear in the air, the little stump of her ponytail jutting up like a tuft of tough grass.

"It's *terrible!*" she called out to me. "Come look! Quick!" I got down on all fours next to her and put my eye up against a crevice between two planks. Nothing, just the green Marne. I started to get up, the position was already straining my joints, but she said: "No, stay there! A barge is coming!" I creaked back down on the boards, hoping that we were facing Mecca so that anybody passing by on the bridge would think we were Moslems at prayer and not call the wagon. The barge came up, I looked down at it through the lens of the crevice.

It was *terrible.* The colors of the barge,

black bow, tan sand, red and blue laundry, cream roof, green funnel, black stern, flashed by under my eyes like a film, one color jammed against the other, flicking on and off the screen bounded by the edges of my lens until there was only the turmoil of the barge's wake in the Marne, white turning back into green.

Another barge was just nosing around the bend downstream. I put my head down and watched the scene again, seeing for the first time the way the photographer sees all the time. I would like to get a movie camera on that footbridge at Bry-sur-Marne, I am curious to learn if a machine can see the way she taught me to see.

Chapter 7

THE DIGESTIVE CYCLE

I have gone out with a farmer and a friend in the countryside east of Paris. That is good cycling country; the hills, valleys, and woods of Brie produce landscapes as great as its cheese. There are long steady climbs, then drops of a mile or two when the wind whips by your ears and you hang on to the handlebars for dear life and limb, scarcely daring to twist a wrist to glance at the second hand of your watch to catch the time when you flash by a kilometer post—100 seconds, 90 seconds, 40 kilometers an hour, about 25 m.p.h.—that's flying for old men. I can keep up with them on these outings until the next-to-the-last village on the run, where we stop for a drink, an *apéritif*. Good sturdy Frenchmen that they are, they can down a Pernod without a problem, I sip only a glass of ladylike port wine, yet my legs turn to butter and my ankles to rubber while they leave me far behind.

On shorter runs without competition, I have less trouble. Every so often when I ride down to Poilane's on Rue du Cherche-Midi in Paris to buy a loaf of country bread, I come out of the bakery to find my bicycle gone. The first time this happened, it was a heart-stopping experience, but it was just Pierre Poilane's idea of a joke. He bakes the best country bread in France in a wood-fired oven in a Renaissance cellar in the middle of Paris. He ships it by air to New York, he mails it to customers on vacation, he has ten little trucks delivering it all around Paris and the adjoining suburbs. But only on Rue du Cherche-Midi do you stand a chance of running into Poilane himself and getting an invitation to a drink over on Carrefour de la Croix-Rouge at Au Vieux Saumur. The ritual is always the same, never a word is exchanged; as soon as Poilane makes his entrance, the owner puts a bottle of Sancerre on the table before him. Then friends sit down and the bottle goes round. I have gone through the same ceremony with Poilane at his country place about a dozen miles away in the Chevreuse Valley, where he has an acre of jungle, a shack that should have fallen down twenty years ago, and a cellar that would put a

Rockefeller to envy. Whether from Au Vieux Saumur or the Chevreuse Valley, I always get home somehow. The bike knows the way, I just follow the handlebars.

Whether or not cycling goes with drinking is debatable. Food is another matter, here is the happiest of relationships. I eat to ride, I ride to eat. At the best of moments, I can achieve a perfect balance, consuming just the right amount of calories as I fill up at bakeries, restaurants, or ice-cream parlors. On the road, I can get about twelve miles to a quart of milk and a piece of baker's apple tart. Always buy it from a good baker who makes it in the oven he uses for the bread. Pastry cooks can make apple tarts, but theirs are less rustic, not as substantial. I get along well with French bakers, I eat their apple tarts in winter and their ice cream in summer. I know the little unpretentious ice-cream growers of Paris, local ice creams that have a bouquet and a body of their own. The red-headed Breton girl laughs and reaches for her scoop when I turn up at Duplessis's near the Eiffel Tower where the vanilla and the pineapple are aerial food for elves the day they are fresh from the freezer. In winter, however, the bakers shut down their ice-cream plants in Paris. It would be a hard cruel winter if it were not for Berthillon's on Île Saint-Louis, right where Sully bridge crosses the Seine.

I have often drifted downhill from Montparnasse to Berthillon's after a stint of work for a double sherbet cone—tangerine and grapefruit, the winter flavors. You always know the seasons at Berthillon's by the flavors, a calendar is superfluous. In winter: tangerine, grapefruit, *marrons*

glacés; in summer, melon and *fraises de bois*. These are only some of the seasonal flavors at Berthillon's, there are the regulars as well. The summer flavors are around not much longer than mayflies, for Berthillon's closes in July and August. When the weather gets hot (as it does for two weeks or so), when everything slows to a crawl in Paris, when the Seine is prostrate with the heat, hardly stirring at all, lying exhausted in its bed, then the owners of Berthillon's must sit behind the closed doors of their parlor, their ice-cream parlor, eating blueberry sherbet and caramel ice cream all by themselves.

None of this can be seen from the street. When the owners of Berthillon's close for their well-deserved two months' vacation, they shutter the place up. In the doorway, they hang the wooden plaques bearing the names of their flavors throughout the year. It is a ladder that climbs right up the glass door. Each flavor is a medal, an extra palm on the family's Croix de Guerre. The nameplates of the flavors in the doorway remind me of the bars that soldiers used to add to their badges for shooting—marksman, sharpshooter, expert rifleman. I remember the names only from hearsay, I couldn't hit the wall across the room with a MIRV. During target practice in the Army, my neighbor to the right, my neighbor to the left, my neighbors on the firing line always received a few extra shots on their score sheets.

When I come down to Berthillon's for a double sherbet in winter, I buy the cone inside. In summer, you must wait outside on line; on a cold winter evening there is no one in the shop except the old lady who looks like everyone's grandmother—or the way everyone would like his grandmother to look; her daughter who is the business soul of the place; and Fernand, the waiter, whom I first knew when he was feverishly pumping beer at an Alsatian bistro a block away on Rue Saint-Louis-en-l'Île. He stopped pumping beer just about the time I stopped drinking it, and we both met again at Berthillon's. He doesn't know my name, he calls me "Chicago" to remind me of my American origins. One sees the ice-cream maker but seldom, he is a dark stocky man and I think he must go to bed early because he gets up every morning to go to the markets and buy fresh fruit for his flavors. When I come around in the evening, he probably is taking his nap. Or else the family does not let him be seen in public for fear that he will be kidnapped

and held on some remote island, not Île Saint-Louis, until he gives up his secrets.

"Okay, now we know you make the *poire* so that it tastes more like fresh pears than fresh pears. But how do you get the little pieces of banana scattered so evenly in the *banane*? Come on, sing!" (Like Fernand's, their idea of America and American slang is somewhat dated.)

"Nevair!!!"

And one of the thugs pries his mouth open while the other stuffs in a scoop of Wall's Ice Cream flown over especially from England for this purpose.

On a cold winter night, I say hello to the family with a particularly kind word for the lady who looks like everyone's grandmother. I want to stay on good terms with her because she also runs a hotel on the same premises. My dream, nay, my

wildest flight of gastroerotic fancy is to take a room there American plan, coming downstairs only for sherbets.

Between-meal snacks are not enough to stoke the cyclist. Between snacks, he must watch what he eats, he must make sure that he eats enough so that he will not fall famished somewhere around 110th Street or Garches, his tank empty of calories. I am a fortunate cyclist, my trainer is a lady who used to work for the Michelin family. The first day that Madame Lea Chagot arrived in the house, she saw a Michelin Guide lying on a table and exclaimed: "Oh, that's Monsieur André's book!" She put me in my place that day and I have stayed there ever since, waiting at the table for the wonders that come out of the kitchen.

When we have guests, Madame Lea and I discuss the menu several days in advance. Another dream of mine is to invent the most important guest of all so that she will surpass the unsurpassable; then I will turn up alone and eat it all myself. I would not dare do this to her, she takes her work as seriously as I take mine. Just as an author likes to be published, she prefers to perform for an audience. I realize this, yet it is with great reluctance that I share her with others for, as one guest observed, her cooking just for me is like having the New York Philharmonic for a hall of one.

And so she has devised the biking man's diet, guaranteed to keep anyone in trim. No weighing of portions, no pangs of starvation, no secret yearnings, no need to lock the icebox. It varies infinitely, this diet. I once had a guest stay at the place for five weeks and, as a matter of pride, Madame Lea never repeated herself. There is such a wide range of possibilities, it is so pleasant to talk about them, the words alone bring savor to the tongue. Instead of putting gas into a car, this is what I put into myself. *Quiche lorraine* or fresh shrimp for a start? Shoulder of mutton or trout *meunière* for an entrée? *Bavaroise au chocolat et à la crème vanille* or *tarte Tatin aux pommes* for dessert? I must train to appreciate Madame Lea's art. Between the last clack of my typewriter in the morning and the first course of lunch, I must do my fifteen or twenty miles, spending my strength on the slopes of the Meudon woods or on the banks of the Marne against an east wind, returning sweated, exhausted, wind-torn, ready for resuscitation before a *salade niçoise,* rabbit *à la moutarde,* a light dish of fruit to keep me in shape to go another round of eggs *mimosa,* veal *marengo,* and that greatest dessert of all, the one that Madame Lea reserves for our most honored guests, *mousse au chocolat* covered with a winter overcoat of whipped cream, the dessert known to French cooks as a *nègre en chemise.*

Then after the *nègre en chemise* or the *salade d'oranges* comes the best course of all. Madame Lea emerges from her kitchen and sits down for coffee, bringing her own cup, adding a stiff dash of water so that she will not toss in her bed at night while the recipes race through her head. If the guest meets with her full approval, she will offer a *pousse-café,* either a blueberry liqueur she brought back for me as a gift from a holiday she spent in the Jura or else a swig of the *marc* that the winegrowers make in her native village of Cléry in the smiling Loire valley where I once had the privilege of harvesting grapes with her on her cousin's farm.

It was a good moment in the October sun, we were on our knees next to the heavy vines, Madame Lea on one side, I on the other, our pruning scissors snipped the grape bunches loose. We dumped them into the basket strapped to the back of the cousin's son in for the day, a day off from his city job in a bank. When the basket was full, he marched up a ladder and tipped the grapes into a cart with a big white horse in the shafts. That is how Madame Lea's cousin gets his wine. He always takes a small cask with him when he comes to Paris, he has never drunk store wine in his life.

Madame Lea grew up in Cléry, she roamed the countryside on her bicycle in the days before the First World War. The bicycle took her to school, to the woods of Sologne, to the villages on the other side of the Loire where the Beauce of the golden wheatfields and the gold-loving farmers begins. The bike took her to Amboise many miles away. If she was too tired to pedal back she could always put it aboard the little train that chuffed along the left bank of the Loire until it came to a steep hill, where the passengers had to get out and push it over the top. The bicycle opened Madame Lea's eyes and mind; that was how she first traveled until the day she took a bigger trip, the day she crossed the Loire and took a main-line train to Paris, one of those French steam trains with the locomotives that talked French, *je t'amène, je t'amène*, I'm taking you away, I'm taking you away.

Madame Lea still has her traveling bent. When she leaves me, I fall back on Batifol's, a small restaurant on Rue de Charenton that I found by bicycle while working my

way out to the Marne valley. At Batifol's not so long ago, one could still eat like a king for eleven francs and, for thirteen francs, like an emperor, a king of kings, a playboy of the Western world. At Batifol's I need not stray from my strict cyclist's diet (had any Metrecal lately?), when Madame Lea goes back to her past in Cléry.

The couple who run the service station around the corner confide their children to Batifol. The kiddies take on *mousse au chocolat* while *maman* and *papa* are checking oil, while I linger over my *pêche melba,* just enjoying it, not wondering how the young chef ever got such a feathery quality into his whipped cream. A friend from New York once expressed such wonderment. I said the chef must have used an egg beater. My friend sneered at my jejune explanation; he knew better, such whippedness of cream could be achieved even on Rue de Charenton only with a wire whisk the way it is done at Huyler's right before the eyes of the customer who has stopped in for a little refreshment after a weight-watching dinner shorn of bread, potatoes, and dessert. So we went back to the kitchen to settle the argument. The chef rendered his judgment, revealed his secret: carbon dioxide cartridges, imported from Nutley, New Jersey.

I recalled that incident as I digested the chef's turkey and *crème de marrons* one Christmas Day in Paris, the sun coming in through the steamed windows, picking out the red-and-white checks of the tablecloths, the alternating gray-and-black points of the tiles. Batifol's does not cater to winter sportsmen, its regulars are around at Christmastime. They take their napkins from the numbered pigeonholes in the rack

78

and sit down for the eleven-franc menu beneath the big ultrarealist painting on the back wall: white water in a racing brook, thick grass along the banks where goats graze, and a distant mountain smiling down. This is the lost river valley in Auvergne, where the owner will retire some day, taking his painting with him so that, at night, he can still look at the view he sees from his window by day, so that he can think up new ways to catch trout while his wife thinks up new ways to serve them, a happy active retirement in which no one will suffer boredom, least of all the trout.

Chapter 8

THE ROAD LEVELER

At Easter and Christmas in Paris, the leisurites (as distinguished from the laborites) go away for a week or two with their cars. The life of the city continues without death at every doorstep. Midtown Manhattan does as much work as any place in the world. Ride up the Empire State Building on a clear afternoon, then look back down on the street. There are no cars, just buses, taxis, and trucks going about the city's business. The private cars are all filed away for future reference, pigeonholed in their parking lots until the evening rush. The commuter who drives to Manhattan thinks the city is eternally throttled by cars. Not at all, it breathes almost easily as long as he stays in his office, it is he who throttles it.

Our children grow up in fear. They learn that relative safety lies in getting off the street and into a car. Then the danger becomes more manageable, a knight in armor has more chance than a barefoot peasant against another knight. At least it looks that way, until fear comes from another quarter.

Our knight is afraid to move without his tin armor, he has no strength without his purchased muscles. Outside his car, powerman is like a turtle without a shell. Where he cannot take his car, he is afraid.

He becomes afraid in the city. He fears the wide lifeless avenues where he has destroyed all life. He locks up his car when he drives through the city. He locks himself up; his car is a social compartment, a cell isolated from other cells. This is the disease of Paris that is spreading to American middle-class suburbs. It is a shame, too, we almost made it in America, we came closer than anyone else did. Parisianization is setting in here and there, the automobile that brought us together when we were rural is now rending us as we become urban.

Fear in cities is not just a police problem. Both the overcrowded American city and the undercrowded suburb are artificial communities, their cohesiveness destroyed to a large extent by the automobile. Without such cohesiveness, they do not have the

80

will to police themselves. Their very geography makes it all but impossible for the professional to do a proper job. We can't expect the cops to make Times Square safe twenty-four hours a day for fun-loving pornophiliacs unless they are to put on the same show that the police stage on Rue du Faubourg Saint-Martin near the old Halles in Paris. All the girls are whores there, but every other pimp is a cop in plain clothes.

My American acquaintances always loved to drive down Rue du Faubourg Saint-Martin, watching the street sights from my car as if they were staring through a rigged mirror in a circus. I now take my younger acquaintances through the same quarter by bicycle. The street is full of furtive men, but they are not interested in bicycles. They window-shop past bars and the doorways and the corners where the girls stand at parade rest. In the age of the mini and the bra-burner, it is hard to see how a girl in a door can get the idea across that she is more available than the girl next door, but she manages somehow on Rue du Faubourg Saint-Martin.

The cyclist goes unnoticed here. This is still a workingman's quarter and the bicycle does not clash with it. In Paris not so long ago the workingman used to get around by bicycle. Now, as he looks at us, it reminds him of his younger days; he smiles, perhaps condescendingly, but still he smiles. And then, the bicycle itself is a form of manual labor. The cyclist turns out his miles by hand and foot. He knows sweat and wet; ditchdiggers ducking under canvas feel sorry for him as he sloshes by in a rainstorm, the social barriers come down.

A cyclist with a load of *Le Monde*s on his handlebars asks me how much I paid for my black bike, the one that a bike racer's son made up for me for city riding and occasional country sprinting, not a Ferrari but still an Alfa. I tell him; he thinks I got a good buy. A Portuguese laborer catches me on the squirrel cage at Longchamp; I speed up, we go round together, he asks me where I am riding next Sunday. We have a lot in common, we are both cyclists, we are both foreigners. I sneak up on a young man in the Bois de Vincennes. I get into his slipstream, then I race by him in the hope that he won't be able to get into mine, but he does. He's a salesman, it's not an easy life, he has heard that things are better in America. I give him the embassy's phone number.

On the banks of the Yonne, seventy miles from Paris, I stop to look at the river from a paved section of the towpath. A cyclist, an older man with young blue eyes, is looking at it, too. We talk about the river and our bikes. He lives three miles away along my route. We ride together, he invites me in for a glass of white wine; it comes from a friend, a retired colonel, who grows it himself. We make a date to ride again. He is a coal miner's son from the south of France; he came up to Paris as a mason's helper, a hod carrier. He went into plumbing and came out on top or, at least, high enough to be comfortable. A few apartment houses here and there, a country house, a modest car but a beautiful bicycle, a wide range of reading, the self-educated man who does not stop his education when he stops going to school. It was he who taught me the first law of cycling: on a bicycle, you never have the wind with you—either it is against you or you're having a good day.

He is one of my best friends in France.

When he married off his daughter, I turned up with the photographer, who covered the wedding, starting when the mother dressed the bride. We spent the interlude between the ceremony and the wedding supper at a place on the road to Melun that is a sort of do-it-yourself amusement park. One can have a drink and rent trick bikes, tricycles, pedal-propelled rickshaws, bikes with pentagonal wheels, a tandem with one rider facing forward at the handlebars and the other looking backward and pedaling like hell. No brakes, just screams.

I get along well with French independent craftsmen. Many are cyclists; perhaps it is because they find identity in their work and see no reason to seek it in antiroll bars. Léon was one of the first I knew, he was an electrician in my neighborhood and he lived half a block away. He had been gassed during the First World War but he had enough strength left to cycle about his trade. Though he bought a big Renault for his son-in-law, he stayed on two wheels himself. One day, I saw him setting off with his helper (I prefer the French word, *compagnon*, it's got a guild ring to it), the two of them on their old bikes. He was going to Saint-Denis, a suburb to the north. I didn't believe he'd ever get there. It used to take me nearly an hour to make Saint-Denis by car before the Autoroute du Nord was opened. (Now it only takes ten minutes, but there's hardly anything left of Saint-Denis because the *autoroute* goes spang through the heart of it, eight lanes wide.) I never rode with Léon on those business trips of his. I was not a cyclist in those days, I was running a French Ford V-8. By the time I was on a bike, Léon was off his. The mustard gas and the Gauloises were getting the best of him. He had to have an opera-tion that cost him a lung, but he went on five years or so, using a light motorcycle, working here and there. He had all the money he needed, his work was just his way of living. He had come out of the war with a crushed nose and the skin under his arm crumpled like rumpled onionskin paper, a gas burn that let him in for a lifetime of skin grafts. He died prematurely at seventy-three. Léon was one tough Frenchman. Léon did not look scared when he pedaled through Paris, he had seen worse in the trenches.

Socially, one can go anywhere by bicycle. I once made and lost the acquaintance of a mailman in Copenhagen that way. I caught him while he was delivering the mail and I was riding to some forget-table international conference. He had an unbelievable clunker. Danish bikes are heavy; the highest point in the country is only about a hundred feet above sea level so there's no need for lightweight hill-climbers. When I passed the mailman, I thought nothing of it. Then I heard some blasphemies in Eskimo or Lapp or whatever the local dialect might have been, and he was up to me. The two of us belted away at the pedals, his mailbag flying behind him, my briefcase trying to keep up with me. We had a good time at it, then he got ahead of me. We both laughed and I saw no more of him.

He was a young mailman, that was why he outsprinted me. Biking is like running, the longer the distance, the better the chances of age over beauty. In a Paris bike shop one day, a young American and I got talking and I offered to take him for a ride in the Chevreuse valley. I lent him a bike, purposely a heavy one, but he left me flat on the first hill. "Come on, old man," he told me gently, once he got to the top. Two hours later, I was encouraging him just as gently at every traffic light in Paris where I rested on the handlebars while he crawled up to me. He did some social traveling that day. Under questioning, he admitted he was the son of a former borough president in New York City.

Take automobiles off the street and the pedestrian, too, becomes a friend to his fellowman. This is not always apparent in European shopping streets and night-life quarters closed to traffic so that salesmen and cabaret touts can pick off their game without competition from the cars. I prefer carless places where nobody does any business, places like the new Paris bridge that connects Ile Saint-Louis and Ile de la Cité. It was built wide enough for motor traffic but closed off following protests by the Saint-Louis islanders, an underprivileged lot whose number once included the late Helena Rubinstein. The only wheeled traffic on the bridge is provided by children roller-skating. Whenever I go by, they latch onto my back wheel the way I used to hitch the Eighth Avenue buses. First one kid, then another, then five or six as I slave over the hump of the bridge in the lowest of my ten speeds. My kind of city traffic does not frighten kids, they never miss me when I cross the bridge.

It takes an unusual event to let us realize what we miss in a motor city. A pedestrian mall is not enough, even if we need only bar the car to recognize air once again. Life must be able to jump the bounds of a pedestrian ghetto, it must strike the dominant note as it does when entire towns are given a reprieve from the gas barrage and the tank charges that are their daily lot. At Tréguier in Brittany, a pardon is celebrated every nineteenth of May to honor Saint Yves, patron saint of lawyers, sailors, and Bretons. He can truly work miracles; he clears cars from the streets of Tréguier and the cathedral square the way Saint Patrick drove the snakes from Ireland. Then the square is ablaze with the stands of a market fair; pinwheels catch the sun, bagpipe music comes from a stall selling records. Bells boom out over all this when the procession emerges from the cathedral, women in their sabots, farmers in their Sunday clothes, the pallor of their foreheads marking how they wear their berets in the fields; Saint Yves in wood, borne on two poles, a statue with eyes alive; a flock of choir boys as white and rowdy as geese; then the relics of Saint Yves, his skull in its glass reliquary carried reverentially on the shoulders of important-looking attorneys, one of them in rimless glasses, his round red face as fat as his fees, mouth serious, a broad wink behind the glasses when he sees a friend in the crowd, mouth still serious under the grinning teeth and unwinking eyes of the skull of Saint Yves.

The Bretons carry their saint through the hedgerows to a village a mile and a half away and then back to his resting place in the cathedral. Tréguier is alive, medieval Tréguier is back. You can sit in the cathedral square and lunch on *crêpes* wrapping ham, cheese, eggs, chocolate, the whole show at your feet. An American couple sits at an adjoining table, they are from Los Angeles. Just how bad is that smog?

"Do you see the cathedral? If this were L.A. on a bad day, you wouldn't."

Chapter 9

WHEN PARIS WAS A PEDESTRIAN MALL . . .

The recent political history of France has seen an escalation of fear in the streets, a struggle between cars and pedestrians. Gaullians (a term I use so as not to libel the Gaullists I knew in 1944) take naturally to automobiles. During the Great People's Revolution that brought them to power in May 1958 (May was a sacred month on the Gaullian calendar until May 1968), the streets of Paris were filled after dark with processions of cars fearlessly rapping out on their horns: "DE-GAULLE-AU-POU-VOIR"; dot dash dot dot dot, We Want de Gaulle, cars racing through the night like Paul Revere, shouting their message to the dismounted. They once made the mistake of demonstrating in broad daylight on the Champs-Élysées, rubber-tired jackasses braying slogans in a traffic tie-up. There they were caught, helpless as flies in honey, stuck like elephants in quicksand, by the opposition wielding crowbars against windshields.

They did not make the same mistake twice in 1958. From then on, the Gaullians used their cavalry only when it was surrounded by great masses of infantry, a human wall of flesh and blood and fists protecting *la patrie* and *les windshields*. It was in this order of battle that I saw the Gaullians on one of their nights of triumph. A great mob had surged over Place de la Concorde, up to Concorde bridge leading to the Bourbon palace, home of the corrupt decadent pusillanimous wavering ineffective anarchic French Parliament, the worst form of government that France had ever known with the exception of all the others. Walking through the mob, I came across a patriotic tableau, the spirit of *La Marseillaise,* the *élan* that sank the British at Trafalgar, the brilliance that put Wellington to rout at Waterloo. There, high above the seething crowd like the marines hoisting the star-spangled banner on Iwo Jima, was a pearl-gray Cadillac convertible, four blondes on its cushions. One was holding up a sign on a stick, a simple white sign with black letters: "WORKERS COMMITTEE FOR DE GAULLE."

That was the apogee of the Gaullians. I saw them at their nadir ten years later in May-June 1968 when not a one was to be found in the city of Paris. It was then that the fearless crusaders of the Gaullian press took up their quills to skewer their erstwhile masters, currying the favor of whoever might be their new ones; last-minute Resistance men once more, everyone had a Maoism in his mind as everyone used to have a Jew in his cellar.

At the nadir of the Gaullians, there were no more wheels in the streets of Paris, except for the high-spoked whirring discs of bicycles, mine and others. The polluted auto tide receded first from Boulevard Saint-Michel one night in May. Students were facing the police on Place Edmond Rostand where Boulevard Saint-Michel gathers itself together at the top of the Latin Quarter before tumbling downhill to the Seine, Sorbonne to the right, Lycée St.-Louis (prep school for protesters) to the left, Cluny abbey to the right, Saint Germain-des-Prés to the left, the Seine dead ahead under Saint-Michel bridge where, many a night that May, the police parked their big black buses across the entrance to the bridge. There were no longer enough Gaullians around to traffic-jam the bridge. A way had to be found to stop the Latin Quarter from tumbling down Boulevard Saint-Michel and spilling over the city.

Up on top of Boulevard Saint-Michel, on the other side of Place Edmond Rostand, traffic had been shut off by two successive roadblocks. The first, half a mile away, was set up by the police to keep cars out. The second was run by students a quarter of a mile away to keep the innocent out of trouble. Past their roadblock, a breeze of freedom blew over Boulevard Saint-Michel. The cars were gone, so were the puking buses, the spewing trucks against which the big plane trees wage their losing fight, chlorophyll versus carbon monoxide. Now the plane trees took over, the air was freshly manufactured, to be breathed for the first time by you and you alone.

The oxygen was going to people's heads. They were standing in the middle of the street, talking, not shouting, not waving signs, not throwing slogans, not chanting "Long live me." Others strolled on the sidewalk, watching the new street, Boulevard Saint-Michel transformed into a seashore promenade. Couriers on light motorbikes, helmeted like knights, sped between the front lines on Place Edmond Rostand and the students' roadblock.

Right next to the roadblock, a small crowd thronged around a priest, a conservative priest still wearing his black cassock, who had a portable radio going. Over the radio came a report of what was happening two hundred yards away on Place Edmond Rostand. The news came courtesy of Radio Luxembourg. Reporters in a car parked near the front lines fed the story to their Paris office by radio. It then went out of Paris, out of France, out of French territory to the Duchy of Luxembourg, where it could be broadcast back to the portable radio on Boulevard Saint-Michel to tell the priest and the crowd what was happening on Place Edmond Rostand.

Later, when May began to look serious, the government took away all the channels that Radio Luxembourg reporters had been using to keep in touch with the Paris office as they raced from one flare-up to another. Without their channels, the reporters had to resort to telephones, putting spotters into houses throughout a sector where something seemed likely to happen. Every telephone in the sector would then be cut off, but no one could prove ill intent on the part of the authorities because telephones in France are cut off in every sector every day of the year. The state-owned phone company is not a communications system but a device for collecting taxes. You never get the right number, but the bill never comes to the wrong address.

It must be noted that channels were suddenly restored to reporters from all stations on the day the Gaullians turned out to march up and down the Champs-Élysées. Coverage was complete, the private radios knew which side was ahead. And summer vacations were drawing near. Student protesters were not going to sweat through July and August occupying the Sorbonne while their parents occupied Majorca. The best way to get Maoist students out of

university buildings in Paris is to declare a vacation. In a trice, the occupier is driven back onto the beaches.

That was how the May Revolution ended. Yet the streets had not been ripped up in vain. Fighting tooth and claw, the revolutionaries had clung to their hard-won gains. In one office they wrested a half-hour reduction in their work week from management. Every day, triumphantly, they went home six minutes earlier. They had won their *liberté*.

The French always use months as adjectives, probably because the same things keep happening over and over again in their history and the only way to tell them apart is to use dates. One cannot imagine the French referring to the Civil War, a term which for them is not an event but an endemic state. For the same reason, they call the Franco-Prussian War *la Guerre de 1870* because they have always been warring with the Prussians. It's like the schedule in big-league baseball—there must be a way to know which game you

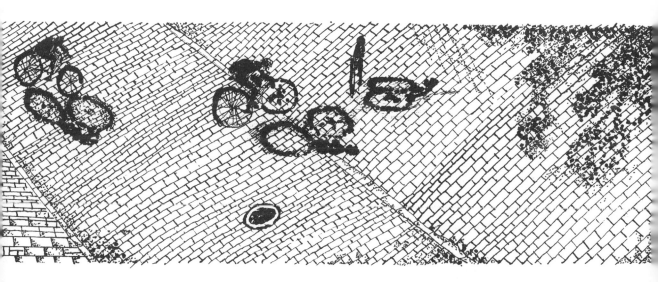

86

have in mind when you start talking about who struck out in the ninth inning with the bases loaded and a 3–2 count. If it was a Gaullian, it was because he had the sun in his eyes, the pitcher was using a spitball salivated with LSD, and the umpire was a crypto-Radical-Socialist. Gaullians never strike out, Gaullians always win. If the scoreboard says they're losing, they get a new scorekeeper. If a judge says they're wrong, they get a new judge. Then the right verdict comes down, the Verdict of 18 June. A street is named Rue du 18 June to the despair of cabdrivers who previously knew it as Rue du 10 Septembre or Boulevard du 30 Fevrier. The day becomes a national holiday until the republic changes and the street is renamed.

Dates are a good way to describe victorious battles in lost wars. We do this ourselves with the War of 1812, the only year in that war when we managed to come anywhere near a tie. People, too, are called by the names of months. There were the Octobrists of Czarist Russia, there are the Aôutiens, the Augustans of Gaullian Paris. The Augustans, a name I like because it has dignity and I am among them, are the Parisians who stay behind to suffer in their empty city from which the insufferable have fled, leaving behind palaces, parks, and boulevards, cafés and avenues aslumber, stretching drowsily, nothing in sight but foreigners touring the most relaxed city in the world.

The May Revolution brought *fraternité* and *égalité* along with *liberté*. One morning on Boulevard Saint-Germain after a nasty night in which a few trucks had been burned in the street, I cycled up to a group milling about the wreckage. It was during those glorious moments of the May Revolution when the revolutionaries had all gone to bed and the police had not yet straightened out the scenery so that it could be re-wrecked the next night.

A little man in overalls was muttering to all within earshot that it was the fault of the foreigners, they had no business coming to France. As usual, I said no one had said that to me on Omaha Beach, neglecting as usual to add that, by the time I got to Omaha Beach, it was as thick with Americans as Jones Beach. A tall man next to me with a well-sculpted face and light-tan skin, no doubt he was from Martinique, took my side in the debate. We recited the Declaration of the Rights of Man, I think he even quoted the Bible. We had the whole *quartier* on our side; the little man in overalls offered to buy us a drink. The Martiniquais worked for a ministry, he said, he was chairman of the action committee, things would never be the same. When the morning-after quarterbacks had refought the riot, when the police started to haul the wrecked trucks away, we shook hands solemnly. We knew we had shared a meaningful moment.

A month later on Boulevard Saint-Germain, I was watching road crews pour a thick layer of tar over the paving stones on the street. No longer would the little sons of the bourgeoisie be able to put up their barricades. This saddened me when I thought of all the synthetic experiences they would now have to seek, even more synthetic than their revolution that had filled time so handily between the end of the Easter holidays when it began and the start of summer vacations when it stopped. The paving stones, laid by hand in a mosaic over a sand base, had given rise to one of the most beautiful of the May musings painted on the city's walls: "UNDER THE PAVING STONES LIES THE BEACH." One afternoon, following a long night on Boulevard Saint-Michel, when even trees had been cut down in an attempt to stop the onrushing Cossacks in their black helmets and plastic shields, I was walking on that beach in the middle of the boulevard. Boul' Mich' was really a mess by now, windows were boarded up, a movie theater had been gutted, residents had been evacuated by their families. Picking my way over the uneven terrain, I encountered two American tourists, a middle-aged couple, simply dressed, wearing big smiles, the only two American tourists in Paris during that month of May. They were saying in their New York high school French to a friendly Frenchman (the species, almost extinct in Paris, came back in May): "This is the way we have always imagined the French."

Yet as I watched the paving crew, I could not help but encourage them. They were making the Latin Quarter a better place to pedal in, a paradise for the cyclist, a glacé surface of black tar laid down as smoothly as pancake makeup. No more teeth-shaking over the paving stones, no more back-breaking between the cracks to get the wheel over the humps going uphill, no more hanging on to the handlebars for dear life while running down, vibrating from the tips of one's fingers to the seat of one's pants as if plugged into a 220-volt socket.

Such were the thoughts that skipped through my mind on Boulevard Saint-Michel as I watched the mementoes of May being wiped out. Some have remained;

there are still no gratings around the Boulevard's trees because gratings can be used to break up even a tarred pavement. Nor is there any railing around the fountain on Place Edmond Rostand, the authorities having decided that it was less dangerous to have small children falling into the fountain than to have large ones ranked against the police, pieces of railing lined up like spears over the plastic lids of plastic garbage cans, shields that could not keep anything out because they cannot even keep garbage in.

And there he was, my comrade-in-words from the month of May, the action committee chairman from the ministry, the man from Martinique who knew neither color nor creed, the freedom fighter. Ah, it was good seeing him among the police and the German tourists who had come to pick up paving stones as souvenirs. It was good to see Monsieur Egalité, it was great to shake the hand of Citoyen Fraternité.

I offered my hand, he looked at me quizzically, coldly. Don't you remember me? The morning on Boulevard Saint-Germain when we got into that wonderful debate about foreigners. "Oh, yes," he said, "the American! The cyclist!" We talked resignedly about the political weather; the barometer was falling, clouds of discouragement could be seen rolling in from every side. The more things change, the more they remain the same.

"No, they don't," he said, with a flash of his old fury, "they're not the same in our ministry." Did the minister call him by his first name? Did he call the minister by his first name? Was he, too, going home six minutes earlier every day? "Don't be childish, you Americans are just overgrown children. This is serious. Before the events of May, our section head used to take the office copy of *Le Monde* home with him every day. He tried it the first time we came back after the general strike. I told him it was the office copy. If he wanted to read a newspaper at home, he would just have to go out and buy one." A pause to let the import sink in. "And now he does."

It was sad but inevitable to see May end as it did in the June of 1968. The revolution had long decayed, it had turned into a leisure pursuit since its start that night on Boulevard Saint-Michel when the traffic stopped roaring by and, instead, the citizens walked and talked in the shadows cast by the plane trees under the street lights. It was hypnotic, it was heady, it was a potion that I shall never forget. It must be worth cycling the world over to find the Holy Grail containing this nectar of reason, the science-fiction world where the dreams of Tom Paine come true.

Up and down we walked that night on Boulevard Saint-Michel before the police were ordered to charge the barricades, down to the front where calm students faced calm riot troops standing at ease, up to the end of the free zone where traffic was being shunted away by the student cops. Each time, we passed beneath a tree where a man was sitting on a branch with a huge red flag. He was waving the flag beneath his feet, watching it ripple in the wind that he created with his arm, for the air was still. He waved it back and forth, slowly and rhythmically, like a human pendulum. I never saw him stop but I suppose he got down from the tree before the police came charging up Boul' Mich' because I did not see him there the

next morning when there was a taste of tear gas in the warm air.

I do not know his final fate. He may have been mobbed for flying his red flag in the wrong quarter—no, not the dreary lanes of posh pushy Passy but the serpentine alleys of the Latin Quarter, the fun fair of plastic cutthroats, instantly inflatable cutpurses and the all-transistorized ghost of François Villon. Fashion awareness is acute there; when Seventh Avenue sneezes, Boul' Mich' huddles in its hair coats.

In May of 1968, red went out. Black came marching in, the black flag of anarchy. Red belonged to the parents' revolution, to the grandparents' revolution that hadn't thrown a bomb since Ought Five. No, the students were not going to the barricades under the red flag. The shock troops of the Party, hardheads who needed no hard hats, kept students a safe distance away the day the Communists were turned out to march in the city of Paris, to turn the Grands Boulevards into a human Long Island Expressway eastbound the night before Rosh Hashonah, a clogged cloaca running from Place de la République to Place de la Bastille, from Place de la Bastille to Saint-Lazare station.

I watched that big Communist march from my bicycle. I could circle it, follow it, precede it, a backwoodsman riding around the redcoats. Hundreds of thousands marched, perhaps half a million or more. The first paraders had already reached their destination and gone home while the tail-enders were still playing cards on the hot asphalt of Place de la République, their red standards furled and stacked. I watched the march from Boulevard de Sébastopol, from Rue de Richelieu, from other streets and avenues that intersected the Grands Boulevards. It was like peering through slits in the side of a tunnel. I could see only short flashes, never an entity, never a unity. I remember nurses in their uniforms only halfway out of the Middle Ages, their signs asking that French hospitals be moved at least that far from the past. None of the signs went much further. Wild-eyed Communists, Red and proud of it, took over the streets of the nation's capital, banners demanding . . . a forty-hour week . . . the right to join a union . . . a chance to negotiate with management. They would have been the dragging sagging Right in the United States during the days of the New Deal.

I found them sad, those great gray masses that rocked, swayed, heaved along the street as if the struck subway lines were back in operation above ground, transporting their inert loads, straphangers without straps, riders without wheels. No one danced, few smiled, there was no tension, just obedient shouting in unison. *At my command . . .* WAVE! Out came a cottonfield, a Mississippi delta of handkerchiefs, up rose the chorus from the ranks: "Adieu, de Gaulle . . . Adieu, de Gaulle . . . Adieu." But at Saint-Lazare station, half a mile from the shaky quaking seat of power in the République, the victorious local version of the Red Army at the end of its long march simply dispersed, melted, vanished, just like the crowds of commuters that arrive at Saint-Lazare station during the morning rush. No one knew where, no one knew how. The march only showed that people as well as traffic could block the streets of Paris.

Yet it gave de Gaulle a stick that he used a few days later to beat the living fear of God into the middle-class middling muddling Parisians. Now things were serious, *la patrie* might or might not have been in danger, de Gaulle certainly was. No more salon chitchat about Yankee hegemony, no time could be wasted on the Anglo-Saxon octopus choking the breath of France, squeezing the sap from her vineyards, covering her sacred soil with an infamous pollution of dollars. No, this was the time for the old bedtime story about the Bolshevik in the closet waiting to get the gold in the mattress. De Gaulle told it like the great grandpa he was, with the tremolo in the right places, the thunder and the threats, the terrible suspense just before the Red witch opens her oven to clap the little Parisian in, the near-relief of the terror that comes when she slams the door shut, the happy ending when de Gaulle arrives in the nick of time to pull the little Parisian out, slightly seared but so much wiser, and to drive the Red witch back into the woods where he can keep her on tap until her services are needed again.

The Communist march to Saint-Lazare station was the last parade that I really watched during May and June of 1968. By that time, demonstrations had sunk into conformity, there was an establishment way of raising hell, a power structure had taken over from street power. In less than six weeks, the movement had grown up and died. I could still remember the birth, the first hesitant steps through the playpen of the Latin Quarter.

One day, a small band, fifty or a hundred, soon they were two hundred, of serious kids marched down Boulevard

90

Saint-Michel. On their momentum, they crossed the Seine. The bridges were empty, the streets on Île de la Cité were clear. They crossed the Seine and entered Boulevard de Sébastopol where it starts on the river, the hard-working hard-selling extension of Boul' Mich' on the Right Bank—no students, no Drugstores, no mod shops, no pubs, just a broad sweep running right up to Gare de l'Est, the great, elegant East station that sits on top of Sebasto' like a god waiting to swallow up another generation of sound solid kind friendly Frenchmen, to ship them off to the grinding mills on the Marne, in Alsace, on the German border.

The kids marched innocently up Boulevard de Sébastopol, carrying the word from Boulevard Saint-Michel to the Arabs and the whores, the shopkeepers and the housewives of the old Halles quarter that was still raising hell all night long every night except Sunday though already on its deathbed, gasping its last breaths for a few more months while work went ahead on the new markets at Rungis south of Paris, just a mile or so away from Orly Airport, strategically placed by the logic of *le plan* in the nexus of the biggest traffic mess in Western Europe.

Planners responsible for *le plan* want to move everything out of the city of Paris so that their friends can buy up the vacant tenements, the deserted market sheds, and mine money out of them, putting up ten or fifteen or twenty stories in the courtyards where once handcarts snored during the day, awaiting their nightly chores. Money grows in the streets of Paris, they are paved with gold if you know the right Gaullian. You buy an old building, where you do not even have the right to polish the brass doorknobs without getting the permission of the Undersecretary of Fine Arts, who has to make sure that you will polish them to exactly the same hue and gleam as all the other brass doorknobs in the neighborhood, classified as an historic quarter. Then you go to the right Gaullian and he changes the classification. Off go the doorknobs to be sold to an antique dealer, down comes the building, up go the cinderblocks and the concrete. Gone are the handcarts, gone are their Arab handlers, stout fellows who could make five or six dollars a night as human truckers, hauling half a ton of vegetables from seller to buyer through the market sheds.

The market people are exiled to the suburbs, the new walls of Paris, weeds of concrete and glass sprouting where green pastures, yellow wheatfields, hand-plucked market gardens grew the year before. At the Sorbonne during May, a poster showed those suburban housing projects as cans for storing labor. The biggest of all, Sarcelles, contains a supply of fifty thousand, who suffer from a disease called Sarcellitis. One symptom, discovered by a weekly catering to readers on the Left Bank Left, is prostitution by housewives who take to their beds to pay the rent. The story sent all the weekly's hand-plucked hand-polished hand-handled readers squealing in horror to their great and good friends about such a state of affairs. In a well-ordered French society with *liberté* and *justice* for all (of which the Left Bank Left is the herald, carrying the good word to the dying farm villages of Île de France, where it gobbles up land for weekend houses, spreading the gospel to

Saint-Tropez where it has driven the fishermen to the hills and the hill people to extinction, wiping them from the face of Provence as the Saracens were never able to do), in such a well-ordered society, it is not necessary for wives to whore for the rent. Husbands pay the rent, leaving wives the time and leisure to widen their circle of friends.

And their kids were marching up Boulevard de Sébastopol. I tagged along behind on my bike, I sprinted ahead. People in the street stopped to watch out of curiosity. They stared at each other uneasily the way city people do when someone makes a spectacle of himself, when a drunk mouths obscenities. Along the sidewalk, an over-forty was striding briskly in a raincoat, he was carrying a briefcase. Every few steps, he would bellow like a brazen bull: "De Gaulle!" And the marching kids would chorus back; "*Assassin!*" Point and counterpoint, priest and congregation, up Boulevard de Sébastopol the leader strode like a pied piper, the kids following him, boys and girls in jeans bringing up the rear, closing in on the stragglers. Such words had not resounded in France for nearly eight years, not since the pathetic putsch of 1961 when three insurgent generals proved they were as incompetent at rebellion as at any other form of action. It was then, when the three generals were the masters of Algiers, that General de Gaulle took to the tube, the terrain of his greatest triumphs, to appeal to his people. "Help me!" he begged. They did and he never forgave them. To punish them for having created him, he placed them under a pall. He put a shroud over their verve, their wit, their *joie de vivre*. They lived like a canary with a black cloth over its cage, never singing because the sun never came out.

"De Gaulle . . . *assassin!*" cried the pied piper and the children. Street cries came back to Paris in May. The last to go had been the old clothes man and the glazier who pedaled slowly under your window on his bicycle, a big pane in the back of his neck. The old cries were gone, so were the old criers. The city heard only the bleat of forbidden car horns when traffic piled up to the point where the herd could moo with none of the individual steers being singled out for branding. Now the cries came back:

"De Gaulle . . . *assassin!*"
"Ten years . . . that's enough!"
"Liberate . . . the Sorbonne!"

When *L'Humanité,* the French Communist Party's organ, as it says under the masthead without specifying which one, when *L'Humanité* said that Dany Cohn-Bendit, the student leader, was a German Jew, his comrades marched along Boulevard Raspail to the chant of:

"We are all . . . German Jews!

The new cries became a new way of speaking, they were the sound track for the slogans on the walls, those truisms written as if to be read in slow motion. "ADVERTISING MANIPULATES" I once saw on a wall on the old scaly flaking side of Rue Saint-Jacques that is due to come down some day when the street is widened to provide a pendant to Boulevard Saint-Michel, to strike the balance so beloved by the French architect, general, planner, politician, husband. Only one lane can now stack up in Rue Saint-Jacques southbound, but Boul' Mich' holds four suppurating ranks of cars. This will never do; down will come half of Rue Saint-Jacques so that proper circulation can be restored to the arteries of the Latin Quarter, so that the throat-ripping, eye-rasping haze now over Boul' Mich' will be spread over Rue Saint-Jacques. Then traffic will be able to speed north on Boul' Mich', turn right at the Seine, turn south on Rue Saint-Jacques until Boulevard du Port-Royal, then right again and back north on Boul' Mich', back and forth, to and fro, round and round we go around the Latin Quarter looking for a place to stop, waiting for the day when the vaults of the Pantheon will be opened and the tombs of the great men exhumed to make room for an underground parking lot.

In May, the walking and the cycling were good in the Latin Quarter. Cars refused to go near it. They balked like dogs yanking at the leash, clawing at the pavement to brake their masters. Their steel souls knew the instinct of self-preservation.

In the Latin Quarter, any innocent car ran the risk of being converted into a barricade or an unguided missile to be sent charging downhill at the serried ranks of cops. Or it could fall into the clutches of the barricade-breaker, that police bulldozer that turned a Renault Floride into a smear of rubber, grease, and tin foil reduced to two dimensions, a monolayer on the sidewalk of Boulevard Saint-Michel.

May had not yet become a sound-and-light show the day I saw my little band of students march up Boulevard de Sébastopol. Ahead of them, police lines were hastily forming at the Réaumur-Sébastopol intersection. The kids kept shouting their slogans. The noise gave them air cover, it laid down a protective rolling barrage. It carried them along, no doubt, as we used to be carried along in the Air Force when we sang as we marched.

The gap between the front ranks of the kids and the police lines was closing fast. I squeezed into it on my bike. I could see that the roadblock was on the far side of the intersection. The kids turned right, just grazing the helmets of the cops, and walked towards Place de la Bastille where another police contingent, like the corner cushion on a billiard table, was waiting to bounce them back at the Seine. The police moved ponderously ahead of the procession with their motorcycles and black buses full of gawking country boys, gendarmes brought into the city to reinforce the local talent.

But when the little parade and the pied piper reached the river, they did not cross back to the Latin Quarter. Instead, they turned east along the Seine, marching down the absolutely deserted streets leading towards Lyon station, the Bercy wine market, the Porte de Charenton, and the city line. A packet of police brought up the rear, escort motorcycles wobbling at the pace of a ragged walk. They moved out of sight, out of hearing. I do not know whatever became of those kids. Perhaps the pied piper took them to the Peripheral Boulevard, where they marched around the gates of Paris, shouting their slogans, waiting for the walls to come down.

What I thought was going to be my most serious brush with the Paris police in May occurred when they were supposed to be picking up anyone who looked suspicious or foreign or suspiciously foreign. I was on my racing bike in the Bois de Boulogne, heading for the Longchamp circuit where the cyclists run for that B.O. Grand Prix. Right before the road that goes around the racetrack, there is an intersection that cannot be negotiated without breaking some kind of law, if not your neck. As I got through it, one of those boxy black Renault police vans that do double duty as paddy wagons and riot patrol cars passed me. I got onto the racetrack road, the police van slowed up. I passed it, then I began to dig at the long flat imperceptible hill on that road, so imperceptible that you have to know it is there or else you start taking your brakes apart, pumping up your tires, or making appointments with your physician. The black police van got on my tail as if it was slipstreaming.

I was being followed by the Paris police. I accelerated, so did the police. I was getting up near the top of that slight grade, right where cyclists who have made the grade park their Opel Commodores and take out their handmade bikes for a lap around the track. The police van drew alongside, the policeman sitting next to the driver rolled down his window. He had a stripe on his uniform, he was a *brigadier,* he had a big florid beefy face and a heavy black moustache (a *brigadier* in the French military hierarchy is the equivalent of a lance-corporal or a private first-class; in the British Army, a brigadier is a brigadier-general and that is one of several reasons why the two countries get into trouble). As the van drove by, the *brigadier* called out to me:

"Quarante!"

Forty kilometers—twenty-five miles—an hour. I shook my head, I indicated that it couldn't be true. *"Si! si!"* said the *brigadier* with a hearty smile of encouragement, pointing to the speedometer of the van. I did not argue with him; never argue with a policeman's speedometer. It was this clocking cop who started a very happy triangle involving me, my bicycle, and the Paris police. At the risk of losing the last Alamo of allies I may have by now, I must state that I get along very well with the police, whether in Paris or New York. Like theirs, my business is in the street; like them, I have to stay there come rain, hail, or high water.

I did not have too much in common with the five or six thousand young demonstrators on bicycles who tied Paris up in April 1972 when they rode *en masse* across the city. I was not among them, I was working in Brittany, but two of my bikes were there, borrowed by a couple of American girls.

I do not know exactly what the Paris bike-in was all about. What I do know is that the following week, on a cold wet day, I was riding a bicycle in the city and, as usual, I was an oddity. Out in the rain, I had only the traffic cops for company. The summer soldiers and the sunshine cyclists were nowhere to be seen.

Chapter 10

IS THIS BUM TRIP REALLY NECESSARY?

Tying up a city like Paris probably does more good than harm to those who make, fuel, or sell automobiles. Pierre Poilane, the baker, got caught in his delivery truck during the demonstration. He burned gas for an hour and a half instead of five minutes. He wore and tore not only his nerves but his crankshaft, clutch lining, spark plugs, fuel pump, camshaft, distributor head, fan belt. That megajam probably took five days off the life of his little Citroën truck; it will bring him five days sooner to his Citroën dealer to replace it.

Biking is a much better way than bike-ins to bring down the horsepower structure. Let's take a few figures out of the air, it's the only place I can get them because MIT has not yet done a computer study for me. It seems there are 61 million cyclists in the United States. That's hard to check, I got it from the *New York Times*. I don't know where they got it, cyclists pay no registration fees, I don't know whether or not they are on the census. Still, I think we can assume that 10 million of them live in

suburbs and cities and that they usually use cars. But what if, individually, like humans, not ants, they decided to bike instead of drive tomorrow? Let's say each does 10 miles. I'm not stacking the deck in my favor with that assumption. In *The Closing Circle,* Barry Commoner quotes traffic studies that show 90 percent of all automobile trips to be 10 miles or less in length. He states that "the mean work-residence travel distance in U.S. metropolitan areas is about five miles for central-city dwellers and about six miles for those living in suburban areas." When our cyclist pedals 10 miles in his day instead of taking his car that gets 20 miles to a gallon, he saves half a gallon of gas. I'll keep the figures round. That's 5 million gallons of gas a day that someone is not selling. How much a gallon? That depends on one's state. Thirty cents? Sold . . . the offer will never be repeated. That makes $1,500,000 less a day for the oil business and the highway business grubstaked by gasoline taxes. Since our 10 million cyclists ride for business and pleasure 300 days a year (another number I use mainly because it's round), this is going to cost Esso and the highway commissioner $450,000,000 a year.

As a gas-saver, the bicycle is in a class by itself. If oilmen knew its potentialities, they would go around stealing bikes instead of worrying about their depletion allowances. Professor Rice, who did all my homework for me in that article he wrote for *Technology Review,* has estimated the cyclist's fuel consumption. I will spare the reader the details—I spared myself most of them —but what he has done, basically, is to convert the car's gasoline consumption and the cyclist's calorie intake into the same measure, the British thermal unit used to express energy. He concludes that a cyclist can get over 1,000 passenger-miles per gallon, an estimate based on the 1,800 extra calories of food that a cyclist must burn (whether in steak, ice cream, or pastry, he does not say) to do 72 miles in a 6-hour day. He compares this with the automobile that gets 40 passenger-miles per gallon (figuring 20 miles to a gallon and 2 persons to a car). Like me, he loads the dice against himself so that the other side can't yell "foul" while it bites, gouges, and groin-kicks. He assumes a 40-pound bike, which is a very weighty assumption. In my own experience, I put out the same effort to do 60 miles a day on a Peugeot touring bike, 90 on a semiracer, and 120 on a Peugeot racer with all the trimmings. I don't want to get into an academic argument with Professor Rice, but I think one could double his figure: 2,000 miles a gallon for a cyclist on a racer or its equivalent. Doubling might even be conserva-

tive: with a friend of mine, I once did 62 miles in 3 hours and 45 minutes, each taking a turn up front against the wind. That's no great feat of cycling, even for two riders with a combined age of ninety-eight, but it's a pretty efficient use of British thermal units.

I hope Professor Rice agrees with me, I agree with everything he says. He can really make the numbers talk. He has estimated that pipelines, inland waterways, and railroad freight used 5.5 billion gallons of petroleum in 1965 to provide 1,250 billion ton-miles of transportation. They consumed only 7 percent of America's transportation energy to account for 60 percent of all transportation, passenger or freight. It is such cold statistics that should make us aware of the labyrinth into which we have blundered. We are told we have to burn gasoline to keep our living standard flying high. Do we live better when trucks haul our freight instead of trains? The biggest con game of all is worked on the underdeveloped countries. We tell them to get into the act, to follow our lead upward on the consumption graphs. We have the effrontery to say to the Bengalis that they will stop sleeping on the sidewalks of Calcutta some day only if we can continue to drive to work, jet to play, and stuff ourselves over the brim.

Our fairy tale of figures hasn't ended. Let's get back to the cyclist who stops driving 10 miles a day. That means he is putting 3,000 miles less a year on his car (we'll let him sleep late on Sundays), call it a third less than normal use. Or our 10 million newly converted cyclists are adding a third to the lives of the cars they own.

They will buy a third fewer cars, that's 3,300,000 cars that won't be made or sold at $2,500 a car (as good a buy as gas at 30 cents a gallon, I'm not cooking the figures), and GM, VW, and BMW are going to be $8,250,000,000 poorer. That's only the start. We're not only going to put the breadwinner on two wheels, we'll do the same for his wife and his teen-agers. Of those 10 million, how many are two-car families? Half? Why not, it's another easy figure, 5 million cars at $2,500 and bang goes another $12,500,000,000.

This is the kind of money that talks. It talks all the more loudly because, in the oil business, the car business, and the highway business, a lot of people are not out just to make a living, they've got to make a killing. They are not going to sit back and accept the kind of return on their money that a savings bank gives. They will fight like hell at first, the way they fought safety glass and safety belts, but what can they do? Amend the Constitution to prohibit the carrying of concealed trouser clips? Decree that no one can ride a bicycle unless preceded by an automobile blowing its horn? Subsidize in-house research by housebroken researchers to prove man was never destined to go more than five miles an hour on fewer than four wheels? Oh, there are some that will, but not the smart ones. They'll put their money elsewhere, they'll get out in time, they always do, perhaps they have already. Be careful, the moneymakers are the taste-makers. Once they place their bets, they fix the race so they won't lose. Is anybody investing in sidewalk cafés, neighborhood bakeries, homemade ice-cream parlors? Who's got a corner on bicycle wrenches?

Where are the blueprints for the calfdozers that can clear a trail just wide enough for two bikes to pass through tract housing? What does your broker say?

This does not mean the end of the automobile. It has its place wherever it can stop and go without getting in anyone's way. Henry Ford built his high-slung Model T for rural America, it really hummed on unpaved country roads. I once rode a sturdy GM wagon over Death Pass in Costa Rica on a leg of the Pan-American Highway that had just opened but was still unpaved, like most roads in Central America. Life flowed down that dirt road, it brought farmers within five hours of their market—five hours instead of three days. The car is fine for rural people, they have always had individual transport. They have always needed it; the city dweller never did. Just because Sancho Panza had a burro, not every Madrileño felt obliged to run one. People in the country have the right to run automobiles; that might even be a way to get more people into the country and out of the cities and suburbs.

Then there is the useful car. I would not dream of depriving Pierre Duval of his little Deux-Chevaux truck that lets him work in a furniture factory at Lanvollon, seven miles from Lanloup, and come home for lunch with leftover wood to run my kitchen stove. Until things are straightened out to the point where Pierre and others like him can earn their living closer to home, they have just as much right as the boss to drive to work. He does not congest that road. If I did not know Pierre, I would not even know it existed. The local Michelin map shows it as a faint white trace and he is one of the few drivers on it. No one could run a bus line on such a route. Pierre needs his little truck.

Cities are a different matter. In big cities that have been around a long time, places like New York or London or Paris, there is hardly any transit problem at all once cars are eliminated. Subways exist, population densities are easily large enough to make bus and trolley lines worthwhile. As for automobiles, call them what they are: wheelchairs for invalids. Electric cars can be permitted to the helpless and the aged. Such cars will be a sign of mercy, not a symbol of strength, they will carry red crosses fore and aft. Can anyone imagine he-men pulling wires to be classified as wheelchair cases or women clawing to be ranked among the over sixty-fives with the right to exercise an electric-car option? Top speed of the electric car: fifteen miles per hour, same as a bike and well above the average of inner-city traffic today. This is a wise limit as only the unfit will be operating cars (not as at present . . .). The R&D of half a century of automotive engineering will not be lost. These cars will be equipped with shock-absorbing bumpers (to protect what they hit as well as what they contain), Grand Prix brakes and radial tires to make sure that the car stops faster than it goes. Nearly all our present headaches about batteries will go away if the electric car imitates the speed and acceleration of a bicycle, not a Porsche.

As for the young of all ages, they will be able to move around their city by bicycle. At their feet, they will have seven-league boots giving them the city speed of the automobile and the flexibility of the pedestrian. They will not be bothered by pack-

ages, a bicycle can carry almost anything (one of the few good things to be said about a minibike is that the more you load it, the more stable it becomes). Their ability to go anywhere and stop anywhere will rework the face of the city. The little fellow will come back, he will not need an acre of parking lot outside his shop. Small businesses, small workshops, small farms no doubt will be the main source of jobs for those now employed by the automobile industry and all its accessories. After all, those are the places the car factories raided to get their labor in the first place.

Some ex-factory hands may stay in the transportation business, they can open bike shops. Here is a true craft industry. It does not require power tools or capital, just a few sets of wrenches and a pair of skilled hands. Bikes need maintaining, there is always something that requires a bit of fiddling, a chance to go down to a bike shop and talk. The right kind of bike mechanics are like shoemakers, they work with their hands in a quiet place while ideas float through their minds. Their conversation is good, so is their work. Some in Europe not only repair bicycles but make them as well. Little fellows buy various parts the way the big fellows do, then they assemble them in a different way and put their own brand on the frame. Supermarkets also sell bikes but I would hate to ask a check-out clerk to change a gear ratio or take up the play in a chainwheel bearing.

The changeover will be gradual, it will come about as our stock of automobiles dwindles. One great advantage of the cars we build is that they become junk in less than ten years. It is extremely easy to re-place them with another system of transportation. During the changeover, our cities and suburbs will still be with us. They cannot be junked as quickly, nor should they be. We will need some way to cover distances on the scale of automobile living. Again, the bike is the answer, it is the taxi to the station or bus stop, where it can be left all day long. Parked bikes take up no room at all. I have counted as many as twenty-two on the ground and hanging from the roof of a small shed outside the town hall of the 12th arrondissement in Paris. They take up less sidewalk space than a subway entrance, they are the equivalent of over a block of parked cars. Keeping an eye on such bike parking lots, perhaps offering services like fixing flats or replacing brake cables, would be a worthwhile occupation for the kind of people fortunate enough to be unfit for the jobs that we are now generating.

Or the commuter can take his bike with him. The old Ninth Avenue El in New York had the right idea. In 1900, it ran bicycle cars with seats on one side and wheel slots on the other. I'm not saying that we should rebuild the Ninth Avenue El, but there is no reason why modern transit systems cannot run the same sort of cars.

Copenhagen has a railroad that serves the city and nearby towns. The doors on the cars are wide enough to let mothers come with baby carriages and park them inside. Passengers can take bicycles aboard, too, there is plenty of open floor space near the doors and away from the seats.

Such cars could be adopted by subways. Maybe they have, for all I know. My son wrote me from New York that he had a flat on his bike way uptown near the Cloisters. He wrecked the tube trying to fix it and he had to take the bike with him in the subway. But not everybody can do that. Carrying present-day bicycles, particularly the forty-pound models sold to Professor Rice and others in the United States, up and down subway stairs could be a heart-stopper. I suggest that we borrow some of that research that got us into space and use it to get us onto cheap lightweight bicycles. A spinoff from the moon landings . . . the bicycle that you can carry under one arm and forget which arm. It's not all that hard, modern racing bikes come in at around eighteen pounds or so. Let NASA go to work on a fifteen-pound minibike. While they're at it, they might try to get some racing technology into everyday cycling: frames, pedals, cranks that stay rigid so that your feet drive the wheels instead of bending the bicycle; tires as light as a racer's tubular that do not blow out every couple of days at eight dollars a blow. There is something wrong with the present-day bicycle industry that reserves its lightest and most efficient mounts for supermen while ordinary people must push around a bicycle's excess weight as well as their own.

Such a minibike could be carried on subways, buses, trains, planes. I am all for it, I do not hold with well-intentioned fellow travelers who are trying to weatherproof the bicycle. You start with a windshield, you add a body, pretty soon the thing weighs so much you need a motor to drive it, you're back with the Model T and we all know where that will get us. I think the answer is to weatherproof the rider. Again, NASA comes to my rescue. I have seen a ten-ounce jacket advertised, rainproof and windproof, that works like a down-to-earth space suit. It is made of nylon bonded to an aluminized skin, one side is warm and one side is cool. Judging from the ad, it is more practical than fashionable, but wait until Cardin gets around to this new medium.

We are not going to achieve the millennium toting bikes in the subway. That is only another intermediate solution; it will keep the subway busy until we find another use for it, like storing wine or growing mushrooms. Cities like New York or Paris or London have a resource that they once used to the fullest and now neglect: water transport. The *bateaux-mouches* hauled fourteen million passengers a year in Paris until the Métro drove them out of business around 1905 or so. They are back only as a tourist attraction, but they still prove that the best way to go through a city is to sail through it. New York, too, had a thriving water transit system for commuters. Before the Brooklyn Bridge was opened, ferries were a pleasant way to come to work in downtown Manhattan from pleasant Brooklyn Heights. Even today, a bike and a rider can move within the city on the Staten Island Ferry, the last of the fleet. But why not run boats along the East and Hudson rivers? They could stop every mile or so and passengers could use their minibikes to go crosstown or to intermediate points. All Manhattan could be covered by a riverboat service, while some stops could serve as junctions for cross-river lines from New Jersey or Brooklyn. Unlike bridges and tunnels, boats offer an almost unlimited number of possible routes for a city laid out like New York.

They have other advantages; they run without frightening children or running over dogs, they're pretty to look at, their big decks are ideal for easy loading and unloading, and they're fast. Hydrofoils, the newest version of the riverboat, skim along at thirty-five miles an hour, hardly making any noise or wake. They are already in use on rivers and coastal seas. I first saw one nearly ten years ago hauling sightseers through Moscow. Waterways are speedways. Some of the Hudson River sidewheelers used to run at twenty miles an hour and I'll bet that the old *Alexander Hamilton,* now a museum piece on the East River, could still beat you uptown during the rush hour. On top of all that, riverboats give work to the kind of people Mark Twain wrote about . . . and they give birth to the kind of books that Mark Twain wrote.

I have not forgotten cities without rivers. Most of them already have artificial rivers, their urban expressways, lanes and lanes of stuffed concrete. Once we start driving cars to extinction, we can use their old habitats (just as they use old railroad lines or canal beds). On a six-lane expressway, we have three lanes on each side at our disposal. Four lanes could be used for two trolley tracks in each direction (express and local) and a bike path, leaving the fifth and sixth free for vestigial truck and automobile traffic at first and for growing vegetables later. On a twelve-lane expressway, there would be that much more space for vegetables, apple orchards, strawberry patches, chicken coops, or rabbit hutches. Instead of poisoning Los Angeles, the expressways could feed it. Exit the trucks, enter the truck gardens. And on your right, trolley cars, not Toonervilles, but high-speed porpoises gliding through the cities and the suburbs, the locals coming out at the exits to drop passengers with minibikes, the expresses leapfrogging crossroads on the cloverleafs. Trolleys are not too heavy for roads engineered to accommodate that public benefactor, the forty-ton highway truck. All the work has been done, we only need to put down the tracks, a mile probably won't run into six figures. Urban trolleys won't pollute when they accelerate, they don't jackknife when they stop, even if they are towing one or two extra cars. As in Boston or Bonn, they can be turned into subway trains when they enter the heart of the city.

The trolley car is the little brother of the electric interurban that was running from town to town at seventy miles an hour two generations ago. It would be a shame to let all of our brand-new interstate express highways go to waste. We could start with an interurban track on one lane and go on from there. The railroads won't holler about unfair competition, they got out of the passenger-hauling business long ago in the United States. Even a four-track interurban would not need all the real estate now filled by the motorways. The land could be planted with trees. In no time at all, the electric interurbans would be whizzing through woods the way the Mistral does between Fontainebleau and Melun on its way into Paris. Our highways *are* an asset once we get the concrete off them, they can reforest the prairies, they can bring chlorophyll into the cities. Grass grows between the ties of abandoned rail lines, it could do a good job of cracking and breaking concrete when we are thru with thruways. But let us give credit where credit is due. The expressways take engines of death off our streets and trails. It would be a shame to throw them away as we have thrown away our railroads and our canals.

The trouble with trolley cars, interurbans, and bicycles is that they exist. No one can go to Washington and come back with a few hundred megabucks to R&D them. Something else is needed, anything else as long as it's new. While I do not think that we should go back to the horse (except for providing safe bar-to-bar transportation for drinkers as it does in Brittany), we must be wary of change for change's sake, the now-classic solution looking for a problem.

The Skybus developed in Pittsburgh is a good case. According to a report by Dr. Joseph Hanlon in the *New Scientist,* it is an electric, rubber-tired vehicle that can be hooked into trains of as many as ten buses to run automatically on an elevated concrete guideway. Its proponents wanted to build a sixty-mile network of Skybus lines in the Pittsburgh area and the first site they proposed was the roadbed of a high-speed trolley line in wealthy South Hills. The Westinghouse Air Brake Company was asked to survey the situation and came up with a report that really hit the fan. I quote Dr. Hanlon:

> *Wabco noted that modern trams [trolleys], similar to those used in Europe but not in the US, had all of the performance capabilities of the Skybus: speed, quietness, climbing ability, rush hour capacity, etc. Further, the report showed that by upgrading the South Hills tramline and running trams on improved trackage of several disused rail lines, the entire 60-mile network could be built for less than the cost of the 11-mile South Hills Skybus. Wabco also noted that in the South*

Hills, the trams could make more frequent stops and have a running time only slightly less than Skybus, which means that most people could reach downtown Pittsburgh more rapidly, by the less expensive system. Finally, Wabco noted, the tramline, too, could be automated at a later date if needed. Thus, one has the difficulty that a traditional wheel on steel rail system is far more appropriate for Pittsburgh than Skybus.

One also has the difficulty that the traditional wheel on steel rail, first used to run carts in coal mines two hundred years ago, can steer a vehicle as effectively as any computerized remote-control-automatic guidance system for rubber-tired vehicles . . . but we know who makes rubber-tired vehicles.

To explain partially what went wrong in Pittsburgh—and, in my opinion, what is going to go wrong in a lot more places—Hanlon quotes Dr. J. Herbert Hollomon, the Provost of MIT:

There are two ways in which new ways of doing things come into being. One is by what is called a push mechanism. You spend a lot of money on new technology and then try to push it into the society and hope, because it is novel or different, that someone will buy the product. It is very seldom that such a system works. It has been very difficult to push nuclear power, for example.

And it would have been a hell of a lot more difficult if the consumer had Los Alamos and Oak Ridge, Hiroshima and Nagasaki added to his electricity bill.

But back to Hanlon and Hollomon:

Unfortunately, Hollomon noted: "most of the efforts having to do with urban transportation have been push mechanisms." A pull mechanism results when an expanding market itself demands innovation. "When we first developed the railroad industry in the United States, there was virtually no support by the federal government of the technology involved, and yet there was a period of enormous inventiveness, of enormous developments in the technology of braking and control systems and of motive power, as a result of the expanding market for rail transit. More often than not, necessity is the mother of invention. When one invents without necessity, he is wasting his time," Hollomon concluded.

There is the necessity, nay, the crying need, to make a living and a killing. It crops out in another *New Scientist* article by Hanlon, in which he describes new PRT (Personal Rapid Transit Systems). Building a PRT runs to $18 million a mile, as expensive as ordinary transit, and not everyone likes the idea of having it outside his window. What it amounts to, really, is an updated rubber-tired Third Avenue El, automated so that small cars can run all night long without added labor costs and, consequently, the company is strikeproof as long as the computer programmers are kept happy. I have seen the thing described as a horizontal automatic elevator, which should augur no good for women traveling alone. There were no law-and-order problems on the unautomated Third Avenue El with a husky guard between every two cars to work the gates and work over hotheads. Unmanned transit would be sheer provocation in the country that has invented airline hijacking.

At the time of the Transpo '72 conference in Washington, two PRT systems were under construction in the United States, one at Morgantown, West Virginia, and the other at the Dallas/Fort Worth Regional Airport. Hanlon commented: "Most of the commercial interest in PRT has been expressed by the aerospace companies; Boeing is building the Morgantown system and Vought Aeronautics the Dallas installation. This industry desperately needs new markets for its technology. . . ."

When the aerospace industry looks desperately for new markets, we should start counting the silverware. Ask the airlines trying to fill their 747s or the ones that will soon be the proud owners of a Concorde or two: onwards and upwards to receivership. At the Dallas/Fort Worth Airport, the industry has succeeded in creating the congestion that it is trying to clear up. The problem is not how to get around an airport that requires a twelve-mile transit system but how to get around without such an airport.

As for Morgantown, the *New Scientist* says that a 3.2-mile system has been planned there to connect the three campuses of West Virginia University. "About 1100 students and faculty members transfer from one campus to another for classes by car (and 17 buses) five times a day. They all crowd onto a two-lane road and must allow 70 minutes for a 1½ mile trip. The PRT should cut transfer time to less than 20 minutes."

Walking would cut it to thirty, biking to ten. I am ready to admit that the campuses

in the West Virginia hills are in a class by themselves. The *New Scientist* says the site was selected "because it tests a number of important features: it has steep grades and sharp curves and must operate in a wide variety of weather including ice and snow." Bikes can negotiate sharp curves, they can climb hills as long as the road is laid out in graceful bends that offer a view of campus hills, valleys, and coeds. Yes, but there's the weather, all that ice and snow. It costs $18 million a mile to lay out a PRT? Would it cost $18,000 a mile to roof a bike path, even with an infrared heating system for cold days?

This isn't my idea. Someone beat me to it long ago with the arcades on Rue de Rivoli in Paris and in the city of Berne, with the roofed galleries in Milan. In any weather, people can walk, stop, shop, and buy, businessmen love arcades. So let's build more, let's get the desperate void out of the wide avenues of Harlem, let's have all-weather girl-watching on the Champs-Élysées. We can win territory back from widened streets, we can roof them out from the building line, protection first for pedestrians and, further out, for cyclists. If we insist on spending money, we could sun-roof streets, we could do a lot for a lot less than $18 million a mile. We won't call them streets, we'll call them RaceWalks for pedestrians who want to travel at three miles an hour and cyclists at ten. Goodyear carries people at 1.5 miles an hour on a conveyor belt that it calls a SpeedWalk.

It's not only aerospace that is infiltrating transit. Ford is one of the companies that are building the driverless rubber-tired vehicles that are called People Movers, apparently to differentiate them from what the automobile industry has been building for seventy years. In the *New Scientist,* Hanlon explains that "the motor manufacturers are also interested because they hope to apply traditional rubber-tired technology and to study the systems as precursors to a future guided private motor car system." Read these lines closely, then read between them. You will be able to drive your own dual-mode car into the city, then onto a rapid transit system. Once upon a time, the rube came to New York and someone sold him the Brooklyn Bridge, nowadays Ford is trying to get him to buy the Independent Subway. But when he gets title to it, the subway car will really be his. Does anyone remember the last year a subway made money?

I do not know how General Motors now feels about the matter. In February 1970, *Fortune* remarked that "General Motors shied away from developing dual-mode because the potential damages in case of an accident would be so great that special legislation limiting liability would be needed." Poor GM . . . can you imagine a guided Corvair going out of control in the Lincoln Tunnel and totaling the New Jersey Turnpike?

Similar efforts are being made to solve urban transit outside the United States. In West Germany, according to David Marks in my precious *New Scientist,* Messerschmitt-Bölkow-Blohm (at least one of those names sounds familiar) have come up with a system that works like a roller coaster and "consists of small plastic cabins, each with two or three comfortable seats and a spacious luggage area, which

automatically follow a fixed track straight to the destination preselected by the passenger without any stops, crossings or changes."

Another German system, based on containerizing people, has been devised by the Research and Development Institute of Friedrich Krupp (now there's a name that *is* familiar) in Essen. Writes Marks: "Krupp engineers envisage all public transport vehicles made up entirely of closely packed standardized one- or two-seat containers. . . . Once again the passenger need do no more than preselect his destination on entering the cabin. When his train or bus arrives, a completely automatic three-stage process begins. First, cabins due to alight are slid out of the vehicle, while those wishing to get in slide forward onto the platform. Next, a general sideways movement [forgive me, Marks, but this reads like a time-and-motion study of the tango] takes place, during which the alighting cabins move off to the next stage of their journey, the cabins still on the train roll forward to fill the gaps left, and the containers on the platform are slid to the rear of the carriage. Finally, the waiting cabins are rolled forward into the train, and the journey can continue." The man who invented that system knew all there is to know about close-order drill.

The more I read about cabins, containers, and PRT's, the more I keep recalling the afternoon when a friend of mine, a freshman medical student at Columbia, showed me the room where the cadavers were kept. They hung on hooks from an overhead monorail, waiting to be rolled out for dissection, chilled and still, smooth as wax. Change the hooks into slings and you have another transit system, the CorpseWay, offering instant removal to the morgue in the event of death en route. Or there are the monorails that the butchers down at the wholesale market on West 14th Street in Manhattan use for sliding sides of beef in and out of trucks. Just one push and half a steer flies over the sidewalk on the MeatWay. Go down there any weekday morning around five o'clock, the butchers will be glad to demonstrate their PRT for you.

I know all this sounds as puerile as I was the day the freshman med student took me through the big freezer at Columbia. Yet it is no more sophomoric than a number of ideas that are getting serious consideration. I ran across a story in the *International Herald Tribune* about a proposal by Hyman Bress, the Canadian violinist, to put a big vacuum tube into the Atlantic four hundred feet down and send passenger rockets through it, running between the United States and Europe in less than an hour. His plan has a number of strong points: the passenger would see only slightly less than from a center row seat in a 747, there would be no atmospheric pollution and, I cannot help but suspect, people flying as often as concert musicians would be spared those little pangs they get at takeoffs and landings when they think how hard they are bucking probability. Reporting on the Bress tube, the *Herald Tribune* states that "technologists of the Atomic Energy Commission, NASA, the U.S. Navy, West Germany's Messerschmitt-Boelkow-Blohm and the U.S. Concrete Pipe Co. agree that, on paper at least, his

ideas are sound." The same old Friends of the Environment that we've been meeting all the while, along with some concrete pipe dreamers. . . .

I have filed the Bress plan away with some other ideas for hauling people the way Tom Sawyer whitewashed fences. I have seen moving pavements which, according to their promoters, are limited to only about a mile in range at ten miles per hour because "most people will stand on such a system for six minutes." I have a drawing that shows six lanes of trucks and cars running high above the street and through buildings, the kind of buildings where everyone knows when a neighbor drops an ashtray . . . or a match into an ashtray. I do not want to mention the names of all the donors to this museum of horrors, I am not too sure what I was writing myself a few years back. I shall confer anonymity upon two fellows who did a systems analysis of city transit and concluded that no conventional subway train could ever average more than thirty-three miles per hour. Stops, they said, cannot be more than a mile apart and passengers cannot stand too much acceleration or braking.

Those poor systems analysts, they never took the E express to Queens, they never changed to a local on their own two feet. They must have grown up in trainless America; they never rode the Tokyo-Osaka line where a bullet train runs every twenty minutes with a local in between. They never wandered around Switzerland on trains that make two-minute connections, plenty of time for riders in one-passenger shoeshod containers to cross the platform.

I once went from Tokyo to Fujiyama, using a suburban train, an express, an inter-urban, a funicular, and an aerial ropeway. I didn't wait more than ten minutes throughout the journey. On another occasion, I grabbed a bullet local out of Tokyo, changed to a branch line and watched in disbelief as trains streamed down that single track, sidestepping each other at every station. On the way out, I rode with three Japanese who, as soon as they saw I was an American, plied me with whiskey and their box lunches. On the way back, I sat next to a schoolgirl who asked me to help her with the pronunciation of a Bizet libretto in French. After she got off, I watched a crowd of golfers and their president who made a speech before he awarded tournament winners their prizes. That was between Yokohama and Tokyo; there is something to be said for travel if one does not do it like a basket case in a mailing tube.

In transportation in and around cities, we have painted ourselves into a corner with the automobile. Most new solutions consist of putting down another coat to land in another corner. Cars have given us ghastly cities; conveyor belts or guided baby carriages are ways to keep them ghastly. Instead of blundering along the same path, let's try a new one. Scrape away the recent veneer of our cities and you discover they are interlinked villages, the courtyards and quarters of Paris, communities that once were self-contained and yet capable of engaging in fruitful commerce with their neighbors, giving and taking rather than consuming. In New York, Chinatown is certainly such a community, Yorktown has the makings of one.

The city could become a series of China-towns linked by clean transit or bicycles for those who prefer to go their own ways. I don't believe in unique uniform solutions, the history of the automobile need not be repeated. We must adapt our transit systems to our way of life, not our way of life to our transit systems. When the premium is taken off what Lewis Mumford calls the megamachine, our cities will necessarily evolve. This time, the animus for such an evolution must come from the bottom, not from the top.

Our suburbs are different. Many never were communities, they were originally built as pleasant places to live and they still are, at least in the quality of their housing compared to what big cities can offer. Let people keep their houses, let occupations spring up among them. Total planning isn't needed, just some intelligent zoning and tax breaks for the right people instead of the wrong ones. Once suburbia comes out of its fortresses and doffs its gas masks, small stores and workshops would spring up naturally within easy cycling distance, instead of a shopping center in Outer Mongolia.

What is easy cycling distance? That depends on whom you ask. Someone in Paris told me recently he was too old and fat to bike to work, he lives a mile and a half from his office and he's fifty-two. Madame Perrette, a retired nurse who sometimes pinch-hits for my concierge, is certainly older, she reminds me of a grandmother of mine—she rides around Paris with a speedometer on her bike and she tells me that she clocked three thousand miles in eight months.

At Lanloup, as far as I can determine,

the oldest of the cyclists on the road is Mme. Léonie Medus. I saw her one Wednesday bucking the north wind on Route National 786 on her way back from market at Plouha three miles away. She is eighty. Or there is Mme. Anaïs Ferlicot, widow of a boatswain who spent his life at sea on a French cablelayer. Madame Anaïs lives a mile and a half outside Lanloup and the nearest shop. She cycles into the village to do some of her buying, she rides two miles to the bigger town of Plehedel for the rest of it. Or she can buy from the grocer and the fisherman's wife who come around the country with their little trucks, selling from the back ends. Here, with a rational use of the internal combustion engine and an instant-starting bicycle, we find an an-

swer to transportation in a community with somewhat the same distances as an American suburb.

Her wheels don't cost Madame Anaïs very much. She is thinking of getting a new bicycle after eight years' use of the old one. A new one would cost her 280 francs, the dealer has offered her 140 francs for the old one. That's $2.80 a year in depreciation. After eight years, she blew out a rear tire and she had to get a new one. I helped her change it and she gave me a fresh head of lettuce for my services. I suppose that the lettuce must be counted in the running costs of the bicycle.

I met a Breton who does better. At seventy-nine, François Marie Richard lives a mile and a half outside the town of

Ploezal. He has seen the world, he has been to New York on the *France*—not this one, the one before, a coal-burner, he stoked her over the ocean from 1911 to 1913. He is an oak of a man, he still rides Victorine into town. Victorine is not a horse, it's a bicycle that he has had for seventeen years. He ran Victorine's predecessor for thirty-four years.

These old people work their gardens, they raise a few chickens, they fatten up a few rabbits, they are busy from dawn to dusk. Their houses have never changed except for the addition of refrigerators and bottled-gas stoves. Their water comes from outside wells, they heat with wood and coal. Old age is beautiful in the Breton countryside, these cycling people can live in homes, not nursing homes.

Unlike many parts of France, where farmers live in villages and go out to work in their fields, the Bretons build their houses on their land. The villages themselves appear small, they are dwarfed by their churches. Inhabitants are scattered all around the periphery on good single-lane roads that enable women to use bicycles the way American housewives use cars, thereby getting not only transportation but exercise and the beauty treatment of fresh air and clear rain.

Not only do the Breton cyclists live, they live well and enjoy it. About the time I was finishing this chapter, I headed out of Lanloup one morning on the steep hill behind the church. I took it easily on my eight-speed. Two ladies were walking up their one-speeds. I got off and talked to them. One was seventy-two, she had gone back to the bicycle after giving her Velosolex to her niece. The other, who would admit only that she was old enough to be my mother, was riding a bike that weighed in somewhere between a Mack truck and a Sherman tank. It was easy to see why, it had been originally motorized, now the lady was pedaling it. I asked her what had happened to the motor. Did it wear out?

"No," she said, "I just took it off one day because I wanted to see more."

Chapter 11

FLYING BLIND

Towards the end of my stay in Lanloup, I had to take some friends to an airport at Saint-Brieuc, the nearest town that might go so far as to call itself a city. They missed their plane for Paris, where they had a connection for London and Miami. It was too late to make Paris by train, it was too early to roust out the local air taxi–driver; it was either too early or too late to do anything. A pilot working for a small airline took pity on us. He said he could fly them to Jersey, one of the Channel Islands, only twenty-five minutes away, where they could catch a flight to London. He had time to make the round trip with his little twin-engined plane before going out on his next run. The only trouble was the price. It bothered him because it was too high. He didn't own the plane, he was just the pilot.

My friends calculated the cost of riding to Paris and spending a day there, and decided that the price wasn't all that high. The pilot, who probably wanted to make sure that we got our money's worth, invited me along for the ride to Jersey and back.

I ran outside the airport gate and locked the car, then we were in the plane. The pilot warmed the engines up, we sped down the asphalted runway, probably the safest stretch of road in Brittany on that Saturday morning, and we were airborne. We soared over the hedgerows of the farms next to the airport and tipped a wing at the city of Saint-Brieuc with its three miles of super-highway, its handful of high rises and supermarkets that give its inhabitants the illusion that they are not three hundred miles from Paris.

Then we were above the sea. It ran black under the clouds that had seldom left that Channel coast of Brittany during the time I spent there, the clouds that Merlin the magician sends over his country to keep it as pure as Galahad's heart. The sea looked calm, except for breakers on some offshore shoals, but a green freighter pitched heavily as she made her way west. She seemed to be sitting in a puddle of foam. I started to regret all that sharp air down at the wave-tops that we were missing and it was all over. Jersey lay ahead, basking in the sun, the Tahiti of the North, the pilot told us jokingly. He came in so smoothly that we were well on the ground long before I realized we had landed. We taxied up to the terminal, I got out to help unload my friends' bags and to exchange a few words of English with an Englishman, then we were back on the runway and airborne for Saint-Brieuc. In the copilot's seat, I had a choice between the din of the engines and the gibberish on the headphones, first in English, then in French as we neared the mainland. We landed at Saint-Brieuc, drenched as usual, and I drove back to Lanloup.

The adventure was over, yet was it an adventure? It left me numb and weary, I could not work that morning. I had to take a nap. I only started to wake up that afternoon when I took my bike to Paimpol to buy some country bread from a baker near the railroad station. I could breathe the blue sky, the sounds in the hedgerows were not the clatter of propellers, my feet pushed down on the pedals or pulled up on the toe clamps. I did not have to try to keep them out of the way of rudder pedals. I was alive, I wasn't just watching live 3-D television on a panoramic screen. I shall be forever grateful to my friends and the pilot of that little plane for my hop to Jersey, but I traveled so much more on the bike from Lanloup to Paimpol via Plehedel, Kerfot, and Saint-Yves.

I think this is so because airport-to-airport travel and superhighway travel and so much travel today is horizontal. We are always in the same layer. We are like the great fish that, according to some oceanographers, travel from the Arctic to the Antarctic in water that is always of the same temperature, going through the tropics at abyssal depths, never changing their environment despite the thousands of miles they put behind them. We go from Holiday Inn to Hilton, from Hilton to Inter-Continental, we never leave home, we are like the kings of France who traveled from castle to castle with their courts—and we know what happened to the kings of France. Once there was some satisfaction to this, airports were not much bigger than the runway at Saint-Brieuc and planes slipped in and out unobtrusively as we had done on Jersey. But the faster we go as we pursue happiness, the less chance we seem to have to catch it. The *Saturday Review* once quoted Blaine Cooke, a senior vice-president for marketing services for TWA:

Have you ever gone to Kennedy, stood in the International Arrivals Building, watched people come through from the customs and whatnot out in the concourse areas? Now most of them, like 70 per cent of them or so, are people who have just come back from vacation and what you should expect to see . . . is a uniform array of smiling happy faces. . . . But you see a distressingly large number of people who look harassed and sort of overdone, people who look almost as though they were glad the goddamned thing is over, you know.

I once flew from Paris to Helsinki with stops at Amsterdam and Hamburg. I was in a Caravelle without inflight movies, on-board stereo, or multigowned hostesses to pass the time away. There was nothing to do but read. I sat in the obsolescent bird grinding its way at twenty-nine thousand feet from Hamburg to Helsinki, my knees jammed against my chin. This was the commuter's version, no doubt intended to squeeze the last franc or finmark from the aging craft before it finally gave way to metal fatigue.

I read *Farewell Victoria,* by T. H. White as the lady next to me took her carton of Marlboros and her flask of Ballantine's from the flaxen-haired Finnish hostess who announced our stops in four languages. I read White wailing how Edward VII had driven a motor car, thereby bursting the bounds of the English country as the limit to daily travel. It was Edward VII who was finally responsible for sending me skittering through the sky from Paris to Helsinki on a long Sunday afternoon. I wished that I had the time to cycle from Paris to Helsinki, to load my wheels onto a schooner that would ferry me across the Baltic. Then I could have learned the way from Paris to Helsinki by the touch of my feet. Then I could have atoned for the crime of Edward VII, I could have made my trip in a chain of days an English county long, stitching them together from Paris to Helsinki.

If we traveled like that, we would get more than the same image moving from one airport to the next. Fifteen minutes in Amsterdam, time to take the Travelator from Gate 26 to Gate 33 and back again, to watch the planes sliding by slowly behind the big glass walls. Amsterdam is a plain, stiff terminal, halfway between the ornateness of Orly—that complex of department stores, boutiques, snack bars, restaurants, art galleries where getting on and off airplanes is only incidental and most of the time inconvenient and where the main source of income comes from the parking and entrance fees paid by the Parisians to see their new Versailles—and the airbus stops of America where air travel is classless travel. Amsterdam was only a water stop for us on the way to Helsinki, fifteen minutes, a chance to drink a Schweppes in Holland and urinate it in Hamburg forty minutes away.

Airports are getting seamier, even in Europe. There was a lady in the men's washroom at Hamburg airport, a little saucer filled with coins on the table in front of her to remind you that someone had to change the towels and fill the soap machines. There was one, too, at Orly airport. Business must be getting better in these ground washrooms now that the jets have speeded flights to the point where there is no time to use their airborne comfort facilities. Soon, no doubt, there will be stand-up urinals on the planes. It must hurt the operators of the commuter Caravelle to see all that space going to waste in the underoccupied johns, to know all that money is going unmade. There must be a better way. One could rotate passengers through the toilets, thereby giving them a chance to move around, to make acquaintances. Or else one could put potties under their seats to dispose of all waste products once the intrepid Phileas Fogg, the latter-day Marco Polo, has been fed from some kind of a pipeline, conveyor belt, over his head. He will never have to move, he will perhaps be transported from aircraft to Travelator to destination all the while keeping his safety belt loosely buckled, occupying the same seat all his life until he arrives at the gates of heaven to be greeted by houris, hostesses flashing their porcelain smiles, catering to his every wish as long as he suppresses every whim while he sits through eternity catching oldies on Channel Infinity.

I know another way to reach heaven. Just stay on the Empress' Road after Marnes-la-Coquette. Follow it all the way to Picardy Hill, cross a main highway and veer left almost at once into a forest lane. It runs past a farmhouse and a few pastures that somehow have been allowed to live almost within sight of the Eiffel Tower but out of sight of drivers on the Autoroute de l'Ouest that runs behind a screen of trees so that nothing can distract the Parisian as he heads a hundred miles out for a glimpse of a farmhouse and a few pastures.

Ideally, all traveling should be done as a gradual spread, an apprehension of territory from a starting point, perhaps one's birthplace as it was in the days before the wheel or, to be more accurate, before wheeled transport became available to all. Then one traveled in ever-increasing circles, combing, mowing, cropping everything within the circle like the cows that farmers attach to a stake. Gradually, the radius of the tether was lengthened so that, at the end of a lifetime, one was perhaps ten or twenty miles from home plate, but with no shadow zone inside the perimeter of the circle. Then one knew one's world like the ant and the bumblebee, the sniffing dog or the munching cow.

In those days before nearly everyone was in a chair on wheels destined to put him before his time into a wheelchair, in those days only a few toured. The others could travel by successive states of being in different places, no blur of images melting into each other like Dali's watches. Each journey was a Bayeux tapestry, a detailed canvas of minutiae, some even carved in bas-relief, not a strip of frames flicking through the movie projector faster and faster until *Gone With the Wind* becomes a ten-second spot, until the Atlantic with its mountain ranges of combers, its fields of foam, is nothing but a whoosh of Concorde riding on its smoke, smell, and sonic bang.

I have worked both sides of this travel street. I have whiffed a cognac in a Constellation between Calcutta and Bangkok and then I was grateful for the capsule of my American civilization that Pan American had provided me after the city of Calcutta, an animated cartoon by Hieronymus Bosch. I can remember a cow trotting purposefully alongside the bus that took us out to the airport, perhaps even the sacred cows had enough of Calcutta, o Calcutta, o *sacré vache*. I have overflown the Aegean at two thousand feet, I have landed in grass at Skopje; I once flew out of an airstrip next to a Colombian steel mill with the pilot of the company's DC-3 putting on all power and the priest sitting next to me putting on all prayer, both of them getting us over the clump of trees that marked the end of the strip.

There is always that happy moment when the medium has not yet changed the message, when an aircraft got you from one real place to another, when an automobile just went faster than oxen or horses over the same roads. That is a privileged moment, it can never last, the laws of diminishing enjoyment must come into play. Only ships and trains are relatively immune. The sea quickly heals the gash left by a steamer's wake, the night and the silence take over after a train has gone by.

If the line is not electrified, then grassy cuts and embankments can join the natural relief for mile after empty mile, the roadbed itself a scar as faint as the ones left by good surgeons. Railroad builders were good surgeons. Unlike the highwaymen, they did not kill the patient by trying to show their skill in unnecessary major operations.

Now that the moment is gone for me, my collection of airline bags gathers dust in closets, mementoes of the days when I got a new bag with every flight, the days when the Organization sent me traveling first class. Those days ended when the Kennedys came to Washington and insisted on everyone, particularly kith, kin, and kinlaws, traveling economy on official business for the benefit of photographers. So the bags molder in closets with my memories while I travel by the Nord Express, the Scandinavia Express, the Phocéen, the Night Ferry, the Lake Shore Limited, too. All that's left of the New York Central service between Albany and New York is the names of a few trains. The diner is a standup counter, a Nedick's on wheels, a rolling Riker's, the coaches are the same as the ones I knew in my youth and so are the conductors, but both are a little creakier. The roadbed has not been taking all this lying down. It rears on its haunches, it arches its back, the train jumps, the bogies boggle, it's like riding a camel up and down over the dunes. I once rode into the Sahara at seventy miles an hour in a Peugeot 403 over a track of corrugated earth, but it was less like cameling than the Penn Central on the banks of the Hudson between Albany and Poughkeepsie, mist hiding the opposite shore, hangered coats dancing to the music of the diesel's horn.

Not only do European trains run horizontally instead of up and down, but they always have baggage cars and luggage racks that enable you to take a bicycle along. I understand that in West Germany and Holland people rent bikes at stations, leaving them at other stations. I have never tried this but it sounds like a fine idea. I am for all kinds of ideas, a new one for every new situation. All-purpose vehicles lead to no purpose, we take the kids to school in the Olds wagon that we drive to Los Angeles. In the old days, no one ever ran the 20th Century Limited on the tracks of the 42nd Street Crosstown, but we had no computers in the old days.

The advantages of using your own bike is that you have a taxi in your pocket when you travel by train. I have gone to Bordeaux and Saarbrücken from Paris, riding down to the station on a folding bike and putting it into the compartment where it sat over my fellow passengers' heads. They did not know that the damn thing weighed thirty-five pounds, but I did, and I sweated blue until I got it strapped into place. I have since traded it in for a take-apart model that is easier to stow and also easier to carry because the load can be shared by two hands.

Once on a New Year's Eve, I took a trip to London on the night ferry from Paris with the photographer. We pedaled up to the *wagons-lits* at Gare du Nord in Paris. The conductor looked at us, he asked us where we intended to put those bicycles. "In ze pockette," said the photographer, talking English to him so that he would take her for a foreigner. We did wedge them into the compartment before the train started for Dunkirk, where our sleeping cars would go aboard a ship to Dover. The night ferry is my favorite travel experience. In one night it offers the Orient Express, the *Queen Mary,* and the Flying Scotsman: French train, Channel crossing, British train, a breakfast at sea, another in England.

On the ferry, the crew had celebrated New Year's Eve on a previous voyage a few hours before. Mistletoe was swaying in the main salon or, perhaps, it stayed still, stabilized, while the ship rolled in the swell, her starboard side bared to the north wind. In the salon, two men were asleep in armchairs, their heads wrapped in their scarves to keep out the light. They might have been decapitated, one had his scarf tied in a giant necktie knot with only thin air above it. Their legs were crossed on the edges of their chairs, their umbrellas were crossed on the edge of their table, on the table two half-empty beer glasses, two cans of Ballantine's, one bottle of perfume, probably, wrapped in green-and-white-striped paper, a bowler hat planted on top of the package. The photographer was planted against the far wall, trying to sketch it all, kicking herself, kicking me, because we had decided not to bring the cameras on this jaunt to London. She had only the human eye and hand to try to recall a scene that needed a Cartier-Bresson.

At Victoria Station, we pedaled off the train and through customs on our two-wheeled luggage carts. We moved up Regent Street to Oxford Circus, then down New Oxford Street at a slow roll, stopping, window-shopping. We went into a Far West shop in the Far West End. The pho-

tographer tried on a leather coat, fleece-lined, clear golden-white in color. I wanted to buy it, I had to buy it, it would be the saddest day of my life if I didn't buy it, I could go all over London and never find such a coat at such a price for the lady. A good salesman was working on us. I almost felt like buying the coat to reward him for his performance, it had been so long since I had seen such a salesman. But the amount of folding money one can carry on a folding bike is limited. The photographer had to choose between the leather coat and the second-hand clockwork locomotives in the shop we knew near High Holborn Tube Station. The salesman agreed to put the coat aside for an hour, not a minute more, and we slipped through the traffic on Oxford Street to the shop near High Holborn Tube Station. We never saw the coat or the salesman again.

When we returned to Victoria Station at the end of our stay, I had a great carton on the rack over the front wheel. I could hardly keep abreast of the red double-decker bus whose driver had given us directions to Victoria Station. I clung to the handlebars that just peered over the top of the load while we coasted through the night streets of London, their Christmas-season decorations twinkling at no one in particular, perhaps at us and the bus. The carton was full of locomotives, signals, wooden cars, all of them outsize with that poignant look of old artifacts manufactured from pressed steel and cast iron, an imitation of the artisan rather than today's plastics that imitate what had once been manufactured. The carton and the bikes all got into the *wagon-lit* with no trouble; the conductors were on strike that night and there was only a student who kept the heating system going so that the radiators would not freeze. Yet the train was jammed, for the airlines were on strike, too. We locked ourselves into our compartment and never came out until we were in the womb of the cross-Channel ferry. Sleeping inside a compartment inside a train inside a ship, one feels like the smallest of Russian dolls.

That was how I once traveled to Copenhagen on a Mission for the Organization. I brought my old blue bike with me in the baggage car of the Nord Express. The bike was expendable, I stripped it before I entrusted it to the railroad to save *them* the trouble of stripping it. The bike stayed in the baggage car while I slept in a *wagon-lit* with the bike pump, a spare inner tube, and the luggage straps in my suitcase.

I began my journey in the evening with the roominess of farming France outside my window. I gave the porter to understand that if he remembered not to put anyone else in the sleeper compartment that night, I would not forget him the next morning (I can afford to be generous, the Organization pays the fare, it's just the tips that are on me). I cocked my feet up on the table that would lift to reveal a sink, and watched the world whirl by. Stone houses in Île de France, brick to the north, rickety shaft heads of dying Walloon mines, the fires of the Ruhr, gas burning off at refineries, smoke coming from flat-topped girthy towers I had never seen before. Over the Ruhr, a red-orange polluted sunset almost as glorious as the ones over Hoboken and Secaucus.

Night and the sleep of the just, interrupted only by station stops when the banging, slamming hand on my cradle took

a rest and I woke up, surprised by the silence. A short break on the train ferry between Germany and Denmark. Unlike the ship that runs between Dunkirk and Dover, this one did not have a channel of salt water flowing under the *wagons-lits* to wash away their droppings. Otherwise, much the same. A short sea voyage, a change of money, a cup of coffee, bracing air, a walk to windward, then back to the compartment. The trip from London to Paris is much more nautical than this journey through northern Europe where sea and land yield the same horizon, where there are neither cliffs nor beaches, but only green water turning to green grass.

From the train coming into Copenhagen, I could see wheat flattened by the rain. It was like blond hair that had been wetted, brushed, and parted. The eagles they fly high in Mobile, the trains they fly low in Denmark, just between the clouds impaled on village church steeples and the flat flat country between the villages.

The clouds have steamrollered the land here, ironing it out for trains and cyclists. Training in Denmark really is like flying three feet off the ground at seventy miles an hour. Look at the woods. If the trees are young, their trunks vanish, you rush by a canopy standing on a thin haze. If the trees are thick and the sun is out, watch the treetops. Light comes through in pierces and jabs elongated by the speed of the train, a swim of black-and-light that gives away its true nature of leaves and branches and twigs only if you follow it with a rapid swivel of the head, allowing the eyes to catch it for an instant.

The Danish countryside is a delight to the eye. No suburbs, no slurbs, just fairy cottages, thatched roofs, contented cows, empty roads. Nations that are good at putting together countrysides are less gifted for cities (and vice versa). That must explain Copenhagen, where the authorities have made pornography available because so little else is.

It takes a bit of acclimatization, that porno does. You pick up a *Herald-Tribune* at the newsstand of a proper hotel and there's a Sexikon or a Sexpedition or a flyer for a Real Live Show next to it, illustrated, in color, glossy. The Danes are prim in appearance, but the porno is everywhere. A grandmother running a stationery store has a wall full of the stuff, covers splashing coitus and genitalia, God knows what the insides must be like. At night when the newsstands are closed, automatic vending shops sell porno next to Treets Bars, frozen shrimp, Tampax, and forty-watt light bulbs. It is a year-round all-round sex fair in the round.

The word is that sex crimes are down in Denmark and I am wont to believe it. No one can eat a steak after visiting a slaughterhouse, no one could be a peeper here in Copenhagen where one must skulk down alleys, slink along deserted lanes, lurk behind corners to get away from the porno press. It is an interesting test, this ignoble experiment by the Danish government. If it works, sex will die, smothered, saturated, satiated, and, perhaps, love will get a chance again.

When I got off the train at Copenhagen Station, I picked up my blue bike at the customs counter and rode off to the Hotel Minerva where the Organization had booked me a room for the duration of the Conference. There I was informed that the Hotel Minerva had overbooked, I had ridden off to the wrong hotel. I had to change deities, from the Hotel Minerva to the Hotel Apollo.

Apollo was halfway to the Copenhagen airport. Three buildings, Horton's Ice Cream sandwiches upended. Except that Horton's Ice Cream used to come in three flavors, vanilla, chocolate, and strawberry, while these buildings are tasteless, odorless, not to be taken internally, they must be teratogenic, too, but that is to be proven after a generation has lived in them. The buildings probably will not stand for a generation, they will lie down, each filling the open space of mud and parking lots that separates them. Then they will only be two stories high and my eighth-floor window will look straight into the black morass where a Dutch tour bus was parked. This will be an improvement over the void onto which my window opened, a hinged glass wall, one push and you're over the edge of eternity. In the on-season, the hotel is a student's dormitory. It must have been built this way to keep up Denmark's quota of the Scandinavian suicide rate. You don't need a gloomy Sunday or a blue Monday to sail out the window here, all you have to do is wake up in the middle of the night and fumble for the bathroom door without your glasses.

I used to get away from it early in the morning in the hour or so of life I had before the slow death of a Conference in an airless Conference Hall. First I took the bike to the open-air automatic porno-shop-Tampax-vendor-beverage-dispenser for a cup of black coffee. This got me to a bakery where I soon became well known. Without a word, the baker's wife would bring me out a half-liter of milk, then she started to scoop Danish pastry from her tray in obedience to my pointing finger. I would brush the crumbs from my shirt, mop the milk from my jeans, and I was off to the fishing village–seaside resort of Dragør. (I like the authenticity of that ø, you pronounce it with pursed lips; in Copenhagen, even the fire engines shout with an accent.)

One morning, about two miles out on the road to Dragør, I saw a Jaguar with British plates coming the other way, headlights full on. Absent-minded, I thought, he must have been driving all night. A moment later, I got into the fog myself. Another first, I had never ridden a bike in early-morning sea fog. My black sweater was coated with a layer of damp gray wool that looked like my poor frizzled grizzled head, my glasses blurred, thickening the fog all the more. I stuck to the cycle path on the side of the road, secure in the knowledge that I could only crash into or be crashed into by another cyclist, nothing heavier than another cyclist. As I neared Dragør and the sea, the harbor foghorns grew louder, twin musical blasts calling to each other. The foghorns blew for me in my myopia, to keep me from going off the end of the road and onto the rocks as I floated in the mist. In a fog as in darkness, cycling is almost like riding a broomstick, one's connection to the ground is not clear, the result is ectoplasmic or oneiric, all the more so in a place like Dragør that looks like an illustration out of Andersen. The Danes still live in gingerbread houses, they even build new ones by the sea, leaving the glass slabs to foreigners and students.

On the days off that the Conference gave me, I roamed the highways and bikeways around Copenhagen. Once I got to Furesco, a lake north of the city, a public beach in the woods, all lawns, peace, and luxury, a country club for everybody. It was something like the beach on Lake Geneva at Morges in Switzerland, which looks like it was laid out for Bardot but which is yours and mine and ours for one franc fifty Swiss. Everything is bike-sized in Denmark. Dragør is so near to Copenhagen, closer than Harlem to Wall Street, yet so much more remote than Saint-Tropez. It is a lived-in live museum, perhaps a Mystic, Connecticut, without the admission charge and without the sadness of the little houses where there is no life after visiting hours. In Dragør, you can tell the local museum from the other houses. A sign on it says: "MUSEUM."

Back from the lakeside beach, I rode out to Dragør again to put the day to bed. There in the early evening, three or four kids were playing in a big rusty old fishing boat (with grass growing in its hold, don't ask me how). The kids worked winches, leaped from deck to deck, shimmied down the mast, crawled along the boom, long-haired blond little Vikings. More of them were having a wild time with a dockside crane operated by hand cranks. They had lifted one of their number high overhead, dangling him from the hook where he screamed and squealed more in delight than in fear. Later, the kids became still and so did the day. The gray sea and the sky were fused together by an unseemly tropical heat that floated big freighters on its waves, freeing them from the water. The world slowed to the pace of the ships, to my stroll along the pier. Alone, I cycled back to the Apollo.

I had to do my cycling in bits and pieces in Copenhagen. After a day's session at the Conference ended, I hardly had time to do more than ride down to see the mermaid at the harbor entrance. I would lose my sense of time; the sun sets so slowly in Copenhagen in July that it retards one's biological clock. The mermaid reminded me of a girl I knew with her high firm breasts not on speaking terms and her big muscular thighs shaped for swimming. Both the mermaid and that girl were built like seals, they undulate powerfully in the water. Often, I went to look at the rock in the water to see if the girl was still there. Then I would push onward almost to the harbor mouth, wheeling my bicycle, keeping it in check with a pat of my hand on its saddle.

One evening, we went past a yacht basin filled with luxurious craft flying red, yellow, and black flags, all German yachts in fiberglass, stainless steel, plastic foam, and chrome. One Danish boat, an old needle-hulled motor sailer, brought a catch to my throat. Take off the masts, add a stern cabin and she was *Annabelle,* my father's boat, a rakish randy rakehell out of the 1920s that was brought to life again just when I came home from the wars. I do not remember *Annabelle* all that well, I have no sentiment for her, but the sight of her contemporary in the Langelinie basin brought me back to the days when my father was alive, so much alive, wearing his yachting cap, giving us his orders, being that leader of men that he should have been, that he could have been were it not for the accidents of geography and history. When he went to Paris, he never failed to visit the tomb of Napoleon, that other runt on whom fortune had smiled more broadly, and that was the only monument in Paris that my father ever visited.

My bicycle and I swam with the mermaid back across the ocean and over the years to *Annabelle* and my father. It was a fine evening for that sort of traveling. The harbor was calm, the sea stretched fair. I rode along the waterfront. After the yacht basin, I came across a strange ship, white and bulky, sitting squarely on the water. She was American. The pimply sailor at the gangplank told me she was the *South Wind,* a Coast Guard icebreaker going up to Murmansk, from the mermaid to Murmansk, to do oceanographic work in the Arctic with the Russians. I like to talk to Americans like that, to sailors on ships in Copenhagen or Barcelona, to GIs in cars in Paris. I like to hear their accents innocent of any bilinguistics. I like to listen to them talk about what matters to a sailor from Hempstead, Long Island, on gangplank duty. He wanted to know what there was worth doing in Copenhagen, but he was not all that curious. He had twenty letters from his girl friend to answer and, besides, he couldn't leave the ship. I hope that he never got as far as the porno shop on Nyhaven Quay that I spotted on my way to the mermaid. I didn't have a chance to study the window, I just glimpsed posters of boots, whips, and black garter belts as I rode by. Poor porno, it's so self-defeating. What one seeks is down, deep down at the very roots, below the basement. Porno is the antithesis of all this, it is all surface, it is all conscious, oh so self-conscious, the more you take, the further I am sure it leads you from where you are trying to go.

I saw Copenhagen harbor mainly at

sunrise and sunset, before and after the Sessions of the Conference. One morning I was rolling towards the waterfront when I passed a girl cycling in old jeans, older sandals, a shirt half tucked in. She was blond, she looked healthy and simple. I stopped to look at the mermaid, she went by and I passed her again in the little park of Castellet behind the harbor. She smiled, I do not know why, I did not ask, the mermaid was still on my mind. I kept going to the end of the Langelinie dock where the big ships tie up.

The other day, it was the *South Wind*, today it was the *Cabo San Roque*, a white Spanish liner from Seville, her lights still on in the early morning. Behind her lay an incredible steam tug, her stack ten times higher than her hull. Her name looked unpronounceably Scandinavian but she came from Split, the rust of all the seas from the Adriatic to the Baltic on her hull. Then I went back to the *Cabo San Roque*.

It is hard for me to tear my eyes away from the boat deck of a liner. It was there that my father stood when he arrived in New York back from his yearly business trip to Europe. I looked on the boat deck for his black overcoat, his gray hat, his face that exploded into a smile when he saw us. My childhood comes back to me in every seaport; I would hate to be of a generation that will see its childhood in every airport. What filthy places airports are beneath the glass and the soft voices coming from the speakers. Often, I rode past Copenhagen's airport on my way to Dragør and I have an image of silver planes rising on obscene columns of black smoke, their engines and their toilets wide open. They pour smoke taking off, they stream

it landing, they generate a pall as they stand at the end of the runway waiting their turn to go. No, I would not want them in my childhood. I could not feel a kinship as I did that morning with the *Jens Bang,* a sleek black ship that moved into the city along the waterfront at the same pace I was keeping on my blue bicycle.

My time in Copenhagen was drawing to a close, the Conference was reaching the stage where it would discuss its Draft Report. I was able to slip out for a few minutes to replace the bracket holding the headlight on my bicycle. I got a new bracket from an old man who ran a small bicycle repair shop near the Conference Hall. I had to use sign language but he understood. He gave me the bracket, two wrenches, and a screwdriver to install it myself and charged me fifty cents U.S., all without saying a word. While I worked, he had a long conversation with his street sweeper who came by, steering a cart full of leaves and papers. The street sweeper had the look of the man who lives outdoors, who is paid for strolling, a professional boulevardier. He reminded me of the sweeper I saw one morning in the Bois de Vincennes, smoking his pipe, pushing his cart with music coming out of the transistor radio he had hung on the handles.

On the next to the last day, the Conference paused for a break. The delegates were herded into buses to relax, half going north, half going south. I had taken such outings in the past when I had no bicycle, but not this time. I needed the day to restore my aloneness, to get away from the rape of the mind and nerves that occurs in such a Conference. Your head is clamped between earphones as if in a vise, you cannot move, you are held motionless while the words are dumped into your head whether from the original speaker, a disembodied voice whose face is never seen, or from the simultaneous interpreter sewing together the worn tissue of ideas with the same old thread of connective phrases.

I biked away by riding up to Hillerød. I came back through miles of forest with a north wind behind me and no one on any side, no one to look pained as I sang "My country 'tis of thee" to the trees, as I bellowed off-key with the bike skimming past the birches. I scarcely stopped in Copenhagen for *smörrebrod* and pastry, raspberry tarts and whipped cream. I took on five *smörrebrods* and three tarts, I couldn't get much mileage out of that old blue bike even with a following wind. Then I was off to Dragør again to watch the sea roll out to meet the sky. This time it was a hard blue sea, light dancing on its ripples, no trouble telling it from the soft shimmering air. Sailboats fluttered from the pier, a blonde reading a paperback on the afterdeck of a big cabin cruiser smiled at me, I smiled back, we were just telling each other how lucky we both were to be on the dock at Dragør that day in the sun. I watched the ferries come and the coasters steam past, then I had to backtrack, pedal back to my room for my last night at the Hotel Apollo. The next time I saw Dragør, it was the name of the home port of a blue freighter loading potatoes at Tréguier on the coast of Brittany.

I went back to Paris by train, my Mission was over. I have been fortunate, I guess, I have been able to work all over the map. But many can do the same. Let us get back to travel, not tourism, not the ultimate air journey by a converted ABM bursting high over Europe and MIRVing the customers down to their hotels in London, Paris, Palma de Mallorca, Rimini, Estoríl. Travel should become what it was not so long ago, not a way to waste time, not a vacation (the same root as vacate, "f. L *vacare* be empty"), but as the journeymen moved around, meeting their fellow guildsmen everywhere; as the pilgrims did, watching the great towers of the holy cities rise as they conquered the intervening distances with their staffs and feet. I don't say we should go back to going barefoot. I am all for the so-called soft technology (like the bicycle) that lets us make better use of our own strength or draw on nature's resources without eating up the capital.

Time and circumstances have not enabled me to take any long trips exclusively by bike. But I have ridden with others who have. I once served as a guide through the Chevreuse valley for a young man who was getting into shape to make another summer round trip from Paris to Istanbul. He made light of the whole business, he said his main problem was mailing tires ahead to French consulates along the way.

Only on one occasion have I taken the road for more than a day. A friend drove me a hundred and twenty miles west of Paris with a bike and left me in some woods not far from Le Mans. It was early on a Saturday afternoon. On the back rack, I had a toothbrush, a razor, and a pair of jeans so that I could change out of shorts and pass inspection in a hotel. I started back and, after five minutes, I stopped and ducked behind a hedge for the usual reason. Without the movement of the wheels, the accompaniment of the machine that I was energizing myself, I suddenly felt puny. There was nothing but that frame and wheels to get me home. The bike was a semiracer, I could pick it up with one hand, the whole idea seemed idiotic.

That afternoon, I pedaled under a cloud. I ran before a west wind, but I couldn't run fast enough. A steady rain sprayed me all the way, I was under a traveling shower head. I used the most obscure roads I could find on my Michelin map, the kind of roads that have no signs because only the natives are expected to use them. Twice, I took a wrong turning on unmarked intersections and lost two or three miles until I realized something was wrong because I was fighting the wind instead of lazing with it. I was in the Sarthe country that boasts its own version of the Alps. I did not find the hills all that rugged but I toiled on them. There is no ventilation on a bike in a following wind when a hill slows you and you are hunched under a rain cape.

Of the hundred and twenty miles, I planned to do only thirty that afternoon. Around six o'clock, I would have to start looking for a hotel near a main road. The rural lanes on which I rode were so deserted, so depopulated that there wasn't even a café along the way. I knew that if I started room-hunting much later than half past six, everything would be full of travelers tucking in their dinners before tucking in for the night. A car does have one advantage over a bike: as a last resort, you can sleep in it on a rainy night. I lost half an hour looking for a place off the main road. I landed by mistake in a new hotel that had been opened above a gas station but, in the end, I found lodging and a meal in a little market town, where my bicycle spent the night safely in an old stable.

I paid for the room in advance in case I awoke before the hotelkeeper. I did. I was up at six, shaved, toothbrushed, ready for the road at half past six; no, ready to fix a flat front tire. It had not gone all the way flat the night before; with its dying breaths, it had gotten me to a hotel and a bed. Fifteen minutes later, I was on the road, but only until the first bakery, where I coaled on chocolate buns and apple turnovers. You can always enter a country bakery through the back door in the early morning; the baker is pleased to get a little conversation along with a little business. It is not often that he sees others keeping baker's hours.

I got away from the main road and struck east once more, following the thick blue marker pen line on my map. The countryside changed as quickly as if I had Concorded it. The woods, hills, and hedgerows of the Sarthe were gone, so was the rain. I was rolling through the wheatfields of Beauce. I had the road to myself, not a sign of life except for the big hares that I kept starting. A bicycle is a good way to catch animals unawares. It is stealthier than a car, it smells like a human but it moves faster. The hare or the partridge times the cyclist as if he were on foot, he is up to them before they know it. In the wheatfields of Beauce, the hares are big and plentiful. They feed well and you can hear them thump the ground when they run into the fields away from the road. They're smarter than the Breton rabbits near Lanloup that cross in full exposure to get to the other side, right where the fox I saw one morning must be waiting to chase them.

Around Chartres, the wind rose along with the sun, raising my speed and drying me out. At Illiers, the first town, I got hold of a liter of milk, it fueled and cooled me until I cleared the plains and I could take cover from the sun at the outskirts of the forest of Rambouillet. Then my expedition was almost over; I soon got onto roads I had taken on a day's outing. It was all familiar as I returned to Paris through a green tunnel, in leaf almost all the way from the end of Beauce to the end of the Bois de Boulogne. Then I was below the Eiffel Tower and a mile from home, my toothbrush and my razor still strapped to the raincape folded on the back rack of the bicycle.

Chapter 12

TIME IS ON OUR SIDE

The bicycle is a vehicle for revolution. It can destroy the tyranny of the automobile as effectively as the printing press brought down despots of flesh and blood. The revolution will be spontaneous, the sum total of individual revolts like my own. It may have already begun. It will not be organized, the organizers have got us into Organizations, they are responsible for the behavior that Gallup can predict. I want to see a United States where a survey of 2,000 people will indicate the hopes, fears, preferences, loves of 2,000 people, not 200 million, and no one will survey them anymore. New converts are being made and new cohorts are being formed by the hour. Some 12 million bicycles are manufactured and sold every year in the United States. The rest of the West is bound to tag along as it did for blue jeans and wraparound windshields. *Paris-Match* has already featured a little outfit that the Galeries Lafayette suggest for cycling in the Parc de Saint-Cloud. Galeries Lafayette, we are here!

Americans still go around the world spreading the germs of change. Change must come, all the signs point that way. Extinction has overtaken many animals, but no species willingly heads for self-destruction in full awareness of where it is going. We are aware, the canaries are keeling over on all sides. In a *New Yorker* interview, a young woman named Kahn-Tineta Horn, a Mohawk Indian activist, made some remarks that I keep remembering.

The Indians are being asked to be white people and they can't be. They can't be two people at once. They're trying to strip the Indian of his identity. The Indian is different. He can't make it in white society.

If the Indian can't have his ancient feeling of community, if he can't "go on the warpath"—that is, do work that suits him—if he can't go through the old rituals that signify to him he has become a man, then he is emasculated. He's a caged animal. That's why he has so much trouble in the city.

124

Let's not pity the poor Indian, let's pity ourselves. The Indians are getting it in the cities but they're not the only ones, they're just the first ones. I know Bretons, sons of farmers and seamen, who can no longer do work that suits them. They, too, are being driven away from their old rituals. What is happening to them is happening to full-dimensioned human beings the world over whether in the name of development or because it is good for business.

But it's not good for businessmen, they're not all that far removed from the poor Indians. An article in the *Sunday Times* of London speaks about the revival of cycling in Paris. "Middle-aged executives, keen to show that they are *'dynamique,'* have started trying to improve their health by riding to work. It probably doesn't do them much good, since everybody else's cars pollute the Paris air so much that what they gain on the coronaries they lose on the chest diseases." The *Sunday Times* doesn't know its Parisians; they didn't become executives to choose between a lung cancer and an infarctus. Executives make their voices heard everywhere. No one cried very much about spilt oil in offshore drilling until tarry black goo started to decorate beachfront property in Santa Barbara, California, much of it bought, no doubt, by oil executives. They cried, their screams are still being heard.

Obviously, we are not all going to be converted overnight. It took twenty years for automobile registrations in the United States to rise from 8,000 in 1900 to 8 million in 1920 against entrenched interests no stronger than blacksmiths and stable boys. Before we start going the other way,

we must slow down. In *The Gilded Age,* Mark Twain tells of one of those mad steamboat races, using the most advanced technology of the day, that ended as they often did with one boat shattered by an explosion. Her rival's crew started to douse their boilers with buckets of water, there was no stopping her with the head of steam that she had on. There's no stopping us in our tracks, either, we have got to slow down, perhaps as I have slowed from Manhattan to Lanloup (pop. 250).

We are slowing down. Pedestrian malls are spreading over city centers everywhere from Verona to Tokyo. One town, Norwich in England, discovered the virtues of a "foot street" almost by accident. Back in 1965, London Street had to be closed to traffic for six weeks while repairs were carried out on a sewer. Shopkeepers, to their great surprise, found they were doing more business. Without cars, their street was more attractive, even with a sewer being dug up. Since then, Norwich has decided to keep cars out of London Street without waiting for the next big excavation job. They have learned that it is not necessary to burn one's house down to enjoy roast pork.

In 1972, the Organization for Economic Cooperation and Development (OECD to its friends) did a world survey of traffic-free zones.

In Vienna, shop owners reported a 25 to 50 per cent increase in business in the first week after the traffic ban went into effect last December. In Norwich, all but two shops in the exclusion area did more business. Some increase has been reported to be between 15 and 35 per cent; Rouen, in France, between 10 and 15 per cent.

In Tokyo, of 574 shops surveyed, 21 per cent showed an increase in sales, 60 per cent showed no change and 19 per cent reported a decrease. Seventy-four per cent of the merchants interviewed pronounced themselves in favor of the scheme.

We've got a contradiction here. Pedestrian malls are good for business, but they're bad for the automobile business. Does this mean that the automobile business is bad for business? Does this mean that we are being hoaxed, conned, swindled, and hornswoggled by all of our friends who tell us not to touch a hair on Henry Ford's old gray head if we do not wish to see desolation and depression visited upon us and our grandchildren's grandchildren? Ask the OECD, maybe the merchants it interviews are all running head shops. We get contradictions everywhere. Ban the SST, cut out exhaust smoking, shut down the detergent plants and you do people out of jobs, so we are threatened by more or less the same quarters that are busy devising PRT's to do bus drivers and subway motormen out of theirs.

To no one's surprise, the OECD concluded:

In New York City, the closure of Madison Avenue to traffic in the spring of 1971 resulted in a three-fold reduction of carbon monoxide concentration levels. The recently introduced ban on cars in the inner city of Vienna has lowered pollution levels by 70 per cent. In Tokyo and Marseilles, results have been equally impressive.

Too bad that the OECD did not query shopkeepers on the edge of the traffic-free zones. What kind of business were they doing, how did they like trying to make a living in a parking lot, did they, too, want to be freed of traffic? We can see interesting possibilities here, some kind of a seed has been sown. This may be where we are going: away from the shopping center and back to the city center. It's not all that hard, we don't have all that far to go. The foundations of what we have been destroying are still around, we need only build on them anew. The motor city is a big adversary, but it falls hard. It is like the brontosaurus, it wastes all its energy just trying to stand up, it spins its wheels to stay in one place, it has nothing left with which to defend itself. It reminds me of a friend of mine who works for an Organization. He spends hours at his desk, he takes papers home, he receives telephone calls only by appointments made a week in advance. One day he told me: "You know, above a certain level here, people spend all their time holding meetings and writing memos to inform each other of what they are doing. There is absolutely no output."

He could have been describing the city of Paris as it appeared to me on my infrequent visits from Lanloup. I did nothing there, I was exhausted. The energy I saved because I did not have to haul water from the village pump was wasted hauling myself around. Most of the power that such a city uses goes to overcome the friction that it generates. Even by bicycle, I lost time dodging traffic jams, getting out of the way of delivery-truck drivers screaming at pleasure drivers. I had to lift my bike from sidewalk to street over the bumper-to-bumper rank of automobiles outside my door. In the case of cities, big isn't beautiful, it's not even practical. One day, I had to meet a train at Guingamp, a town on the northern side of Brittany, a megalopolis of 11,257. I had no bike, I left the car at the station. Inside of twelve minutes, I had bought some bicycle tape, a typewriter ribbon, two pieces of apple tart (ate them, too), and the French translation of an American book written by a fellow I know. I had never shopped in Guingamp before, I did not know my way around. Except for the typewriter ribbon, I made all my purchases in small family-run shops. My only difficult moment came when I had to cross the intersection of the Pontrieux and the Saint-Brieuc highways, where pedestrians must run a gauntlet of zebra crossings. Otherwise, medieval granite Guingamp was functioning pretty well. I understand that it doesn't during the summer, when the Parisians are traveling, but you should know by now how Parisians travel.

One can shop well in a small town like Guingamp or even in a village like Lanloup where the Duvals' general store sells everything from yogurt to rubber soles for wooden shoes. One can work well there, too. I found I was three times more productive in Lanloup than in Paris. This gain in production is not necessarily limited to writers and other parasites. In Denmark, one sees small machine shops in farm country, turning out precision equipment next to the cows and the chickens. Apparently, they do all right against big-city competition. So does a chemist I met on one of my bike sorties around Copenhagen. I ran into him and his family while they were swimming in a woodland pond and he invited me to his house for tea. He was living in a thatched-roof farmhouse, where he did research on new ways to stick molecules together, sticking as many as fourteen Ph.D heads together on his projects. He was independent of the city, his wife did most of the shopping. Whenever he ran out of shoes, she took an old pair into town for size and came back with a new one. If they fitted, she bought him another pair for a rainy day.

When he wasn't working on his chemistry, he tried to solve the problem of the little bull he had bought to crop his lawn. He was getting his grass cut for nothing, in six months he would be getting his meat, too. The only trouble was that he had second thoughts about getting within range of the bull to move the stake to which it was tethered and he liked it too much to butcher it. He was better as a chemist than as a stockman but, at least, he was trying to do both.

In Brittany, in much of provincial France, there are still people with more than one occupation. A young fisherman at Brehec used to work as a cook in Paimpol, he can always go back to a restaurant if the fishing gets bad. The fishermen at Collioure down near the Spanish border of France grow wine as well, the anchovies they catch will raise a thirst, the Banyuls that they bottle will slake it. The best blood sausage I ever ate in my life was made by a locomotive fireman near Montargis who butchers hogs in his spare time. Serge Vitry, the locomotive engineer who served it to me, grows all the fruit and vegetables needed by himself, his wife, and their three hungry sons. They get their protein from the rabbits he fattens, they can wash it down with cider from his trees, the cider I once saw as fresh apple juice squirting out of the itinerant press that works the countryside around Montargis. When Serge retires in a year or so, he will be able to do any number of things, he knows any number of things. On his obsolete job as a steam locomotive engineer, he managed to escape that breakdown of work into specialized operations that leads to the breakdown of personalities.

I do not know whether to howl with laughter or gnash my teeth with rage when I hear all the cant about how we must choose between the Environment and jobs. Once, there were jobs in Brittany and in the other provinces of France. They were eliminated so that the production lines could be manned and the environment destroyed. It would be so easy for us to change the payoffs so that jobs could be brought back to the countryside and to the sea, so that people could produce once more what they know best, so that their lives would have meaning every day of the year.

I do know that we cannot go all the way back and still take care of the excess population with which we have saddled ourselves. Yields higher than those of traditional farming are needed, bright minds are already working on ways to achieve them without wrecking the land and our lives. Still, I cannot help but think that we should also try to save what we have, to keep countrymen in the country instead of driving them into the city where, twenty years from now, their sons will discover brown rice and grow tomatoes in a backyard. I understand that if manure is properly composted, it will produce enough methane gas to run an automobile. That's a great way to get around; so is riding a horse.

Just how much can we slow down and live well? I've no data, this would be another good research project for some energetic young scientist with, perhaps, a big Ford Foundation grant. Let him try to define "living well"; he could sample people who rent shacks by the beach or who camp on their vacations. Most of us go back to simpler ways when we have a chance to do as we please. That's not enough; we must slow down all year round, not just on Sundays and holidays. It is the automobile that has speeded up our lives, so let's get it out of our lives. The bicycle can get it out of cities, we can let it survive in the country for a while as the Percherons have around Pommerit-le-Vicomte.

Then there is essential traffic. Like trucks. We can't get along without them right away. That means we will have to get along with them for a while. First, let's slow them down to bicycle speed, fifteen miles an hour, wherever a kid can run out in the street. What are more essential, trucks or kids? Then, put in steam engines, put in some kind of silent power, we could even clean up their diesels. In England, diesels are used to haul loads in coal mines without gassing the miners. There is no reason why our streets should be less healthy than coal mines.

In my dream, big trucks would wither away, starting with the ones that haul gasoline to service stations. Then we could go to piggyback and containers, using all that excess railroad capacity we have lying around. I know a double-track line between Chaumont and Saint-Dizier in eastern France where one can take long naps without ever being disturbed. It runs parallel to a two-lane road where the trucks barrel along in an endless train. Those trucks could be hauled by flatcar. They could drive on at Saint-Dizier and drive off at Chaumont. The service could be easily subsidized by money saved on the upkeep of the road.

Such flatcars could keep busy everywhere. Some could also handle electric automobiles used for long trips. When the railroads first began in England, that was how the gentry traveled. They rode in their own carriages on special cars, with the horses in other cars. If some people insist in riding around in containers, then let's handle them that way.

Setting up a rational transportation system would supply jobs for all the automobile workers who may not want to become bicycle dealers. We could build the system tomorrow. I have heard of a young man who has procured maps of all the abandoned rail lines on the east coast of the United States. He has a little gasoline-engined railcar that he hauls around in a big station wagon. He uses it to ride along the old tracks, chugging for miles through wilderness without anyone seeing him. His hobby could come in handy the day we decide once more to move freight around without anyone seeing it.

On that day, we'll still function as we functioned in 1900, with only eight thousand automobiles in the United States, or from Pearl Harbor to V-J Day, when we concentrated on creaming people on battlefields in Europe and Asia instead of on highways at home. We can slow down a long way, but we are not going to come to a standstill. That is another of those windmills that we are supposed to be fighting: the choice between all or nothing, Cadillacs or Calcutta. This is computer thinking: yes-no, on-off, no room in between. That is the way the computer runs, it is not the way the world runs.

It is not the way the Third World runs, either. We tend to take its per capita income figures, then to try to stretch them over a European or an American budget. From that point, it is easy to extrapolate all those underpaid hundreds of millions into the equivalent of an army of hunger marchers waiting to engulf us. This just is not so. The Third World is a semantic invention, it contains far more worlds than the other two. Most of its inhabitants are subsistence farmers (which is another way of saying what certain communes are trying to achieve). Many of them make a living, many of them do not. They need help, but they do not need oil refineries and expressways. Certain of their leaders may say that they do. I think that such leaders, perhaps unwittingly, are taking up the white man's burden. They may not have his skin, but they have his education, his living standards, and his values.

I have walked on the sidewalks of Bombay and Calcutta. These cities are shocking, they are the biggest industrial cities in India. Compared to most of the country, they are highly developed. I have also been in rural Ceylon in a region that lacked both development and hunger. I know what Ceylonese of fifty look like in their sarongs and I also know what Long Beach, Long Island, looks like in bathing suits on a Sunday. Long Beach is in trouble, perhaps rural Ceylon could send some experts over. They should be more qualified than the well-meaning experts I saw twenty-odd years ago among the Tarascan Indians on Lake Pátzcuaro in Mexico. They were to trying to convince people to stop sleeping on the floor and to cook on backyard stoves instead of on smoky open fires inside their houses. The polite Indians never told the experts that the fires warmed the floor and made it fine for sleeping on a cold night in the mountains. People in Calcutta have got far worse problems, but the cowboy approach is not going to help those Indians any more than it did any others.

It is true that I dream. I have been too long in Lanloup where there are still sorcerers around, although, so I was told in the village graveyard, they do not practice any more. Perhaps the retired sorcerers have been casting a few spells over me just as the retired seamen cast a few nets from the little boats they sail out of Brehec on a calm sunny day. We need spells and mystery in our lives, the modern city drives them away and replaces them with drugs and neuroses. Just as the automobile allows us to travel without moving our muscles, drugs let us dream without moving our minds.

The motor city can drive mystery away from Lanloup when summer starts and the migrating birds arrive from Paris, pendulous men and women in their mustard-colored Asconas and Taunuses, yachtsmen coming ashore in hip boots, bright yellow slickers, and stocking caps, they look as if they've been clewing up the topgallants off Tierra del Fuego. It's easy to tell the yachtsmen from the fishermen, the fishermen wear coveralls and look like mechanics.

I wonder where Merlin spends his summers. I suspect he comes to Paris as an Augustan. That may be why I can dream in the Paris of August. I coast hands off down Rue d'Assas on a Sunday morning, the first batch of newly made air comes fresh to me through the grille of the Luxembourg Gardens. The Seine sparkles like all the seas I have ever known, the sky over the Left Bank is as washed and clear as it is over the English Channel between Saint-Brieuc and Jersey. I dream of a Paris year of twelve Augusts.

I dream of the day when we will travel once more on the little wooden passenger coaches that were turned into sheds and summer houses when the branch line closed down at Brehec. I do not know who will be driving the train, perhaps it will be the man who ran a switch engine I once saw outside the old roundhouse at Nogent-sur-Marne that is now dust. From the track, I admired his engine; from the cab, he admired my racing bike. He told me that he came to work himself on a racing bike all the way from Livry-Gargan. Perhaps it was from Brooklyn Heights, it could have been from Dragør, I am not sure. I saw him only once. All I can remember is that he invited me to come aboard his little steam engine for a fireside chat. Its copper pipes gleamed, he opened the firebox door, threw in a shovelful of coal and closed it, all in the same dancing movement.

Then we talked about bicycles.

Lanloup, June 1972

73 74 75   12 11 10 9 8 7 6 5 4 3 2 1